Creating
Android
Applications

DEVELOP AND DESIGN

Chris Haseman

Peachpit
Press

Creating Android Applications: Develop and Design

Chris Haseman

Peachpit Press

1249 Eighth Street
Berkeley, CA 94710
510/524-2178
510/524-2221 (fax)

Find us on the Web at: www.peachpit.com
To report errors, please send a note to errata@peachpit.com
Peachpit Press is a division of Pearson Education.
Copyright © 2012 by Chris Haseman

Editor: Clifford Colby
Development editor: Robyn Thomas
Production editor: Myrna Vladic
Copyeditor: Scout Festa
Technical editor: Jason LeBrun
Cover design: Aren Howell Straiger
Interior design: Mimi Heft
Compositor: Danielle Foster
Indexer: Valerie Haynes Perry

ISBN-13: 978-0-321-78409-4
ISBN-10: 0-321-78409-x

9 8 7 6 5 4 3 2 1

Printed and bound in the United States of America

To my wife, Meghan,
who's made me the teacher, writer, and man I am today.

BIO

Chris Haseman has been writing mobile software in various forms since 2003. He was involved in several large-scale BREW projects, from MMS messaging to Major League Baseball. More recently, he was an early Android engineer behind the doubleTwist media player, and he is now the lead Android developer for the website Tumblr. He's a faculty member of General Assembly in NYC, where he teaches Android development. He lives in Brooklyn, where he constantly debates shaving his beard.

ACKNOWLEDGMENTS

As always, I could spend more pages thanking people than are in the work itself. Here are a few who stand out:

David and Susanne H for their support. Ellen Y. for believing so early that I could do this. JBL for fixing my code. Robyn T. for her patience. Cliff C. for finding me. Scout F. for her tolerance of my grammar. Sharon H. for her harassment IMs. Dan C. for his backing. Edwin and Susan K. for their care. Thomas K. for his subtle and quiet voice. Sparks for his humor. Cotton for "being there." Lee for the place to write. The teams at both Tumblr and doubleTwist for all their encouragement. The Android team at Google for all their hard work. Most of all, Peachpit for giving me the opportunity to write for you.

CONTENTS

INTRODUCTION

If you've got a burning idea for an application that you're dying to share, or if you recognize the power and possibilities of the Android platform, you've come to the right place. This is a short book on an immense topic.

I don't mean to alarm anyone right off the bat here, but let me be honest: Android development is hard. Its architecture is dissimilar to that of many existing platforms (especially other mobile SDKs), there are many traps for beginners to fall into, and the documentation is frequently sparse at best. In exchange for its difficulty, however, Google's Android offers unprecedented power, control, and—yes—responsibility to those who are brave enough to develop for it.

This is where my job comes in. I'm here to make the process of learning to write amazing Android software as simple as possible.

Who am I to ask such things of you? I've been writing mobile software in a professional capacity for more than eight years, and for three of those years, I've been developing software for Android. I've written code that runs on millions of handsets throughout the world. Also, I have a beard. We all know that people with ample facial hair appear to be more authoritative on all subjects.

In return for making this learning process as easy as possible, I ask for a few things:

- **You have a computer.** My third-grade teacher taught me never to take anything for granted; maybe you *don't* have a computer. If you don't already have a computer, you'll need one—preferably a fast one, because the Android emulator and Eclipse can use up a fair amount of resources quickly.

  NOTE: Android is an equal opportunity development platform. While I personally develop on a Mac, you can use any of the three major platforms (Mac, PC, or Linux).

- **You're fluent in Java.** Notice that I say *fluent,* not *expert.* Because you'll be writing usable applications (rather than production libraries, at least to start), I expect you to know the differences between classes and interfaces. You should be able to handle threads and concurrency without batting an eyelash. Further, the more you know about what happens under the hood (in terms of object creation and garbage collection), the faster and better your mobile applications will be.

  Yes, you can get through the book and even put together rudimentary applications without knowing much about the Java programming language.

However, when you encounter problems—in both performance and possibilities—a weak foundation in the programming language may leave you without a solution.

■ **You have boundless patience and endless curiosity.** Your interest in and passion for Android will help you through the difficult subjects covered in this book and let you glide through the easy ones.

Throughout this book, I focus on how to write features, debug problems, and make interesting software. I hope that when you've finished the book, you'll have a firm grasp of the fundamentals of Android software development.

NOTE: If you're more interested in the many "whys" behind Android, this book is a good one to start with, but it won't answer every question you may have.

All right, that's quite enough idle talking. Let's get started.

WHO THIS BOOK IS FOR

This book is for people who have some programming experience and are curious about the wild world of Android development.

WHO THIS BOOK IS NOT FOR

This book is not for people who have never seen a line of Java before. It is also not for expert Android engineers with several applications under their belt.

HOW YOU WILL LEARN

In this book, you'll learn by doing. Each chapter comes with companion sample code and clear, concise instructions for how to build that code for yourself. You'll find the code samples on the book's website (www.peachpit.com/androiddevelopanddesign).

WHAT YOU WILL LEARN

You'll learn the basics of Android development, from creating a project to building scalable UIs that move between tablets and phones.

i

WELCOME TO ANDROID

WELCOME TO ANDROID

Eclipse and the Android SDK are the two major tools you'll use to follow along with the examples in this book. There are, however, a few others you should be aware of that will be very useful now and in your future work with Android. While you may not use all of these tools until you're getting ready to ship an application, it will be helpful to know about them when the need arises.

THE TOOLS

Over the course of this book, you'll work with several tools that will make your life with Google's Android much easier. Here they are in no particular order:

ECLIPSE

Eclipse is the primary tool that I'll be using throughout the book. Google has blessed it as the primary IDE for Android development and has released plug-ins to help. Make sure you get them, because they take all the pain out of creating a project and stepping through your application on the device. You're welcome to use Eclipse as well, or, if you're some sort of command-line junkie, you can follow along with Vim or Emacs if you prefer.

ANDROID SDK

The Android SDK contains all the tools you'll need to develop Android applications from the command line as well as other tools to help you find and diagnose problems and streamline your applications. You can download the Android SDK at http://developer.android.com/sdk/index.html.

ANDROID SDK MANAGER

The Android SDK Manager (found within the SDK tools/ directory) will help you pull down all versions of the SDK as well as a plethora of tools, third-party add-ons, and all things Android. This will be the primary way in which you get new software from Google's headquarters in Mountain View, California.

HIERARCHY VIEWER

This tool will help you track the complex connections between your layouts and views as you build and debug your applications. This viewer can be indispensable when tracking down those hard-to-understand layout issues. You can find this tool in the SDK tools/ directory as hierarchyviewer.

DDMS

DDMS (Dalvik Debug Monitor Server) is your primary way to interface with and debug Android devices. You'll find it in the tools/ directory inside the Android SDK. It does everything from gathering logs, sending mock text messages or locations, and mapping memory allocations to taking screenshots. Eclipse users have a perspective that duplicates, within Eclipse, all the functionality that this stand-alone application offers. This tool is very much the Swiss Army knife of your Android toolkit.

1

GETTING STARTED
WITH **ANDROID**

The first step when building an Android application is installing the tools and the SDK. If you've already
built an Android application, congratulations are in order!
You can skip this chapter and move on to the fundamentals. For
those of you who haven't, you'll get through this busy work before
you can say "Open Handset Alliance" three times quickly.

In this chapter, you'll move quickly through the platform configuration. I'll show you how to download developer files from
Google and the Eclipse project; install and configure the Android
Software Development Kit (SDK) and Eclipse; create and configure
a shiny new Android emulator; start a new Android project; and
run your Android project on your shiny new Android emulator.

DOWNLOADING
DEVELOPER **SOFTWARE**

First, you need to download a few software tools—namely, the Android SDK, the Eclipse integrated development environment (IDE), and the Android plug-in for Eclipse. There are many other tools a developer could use to make Android applications, but I've found that this setup has the fewest hassles and will get you up and running in the least amount of time.

THE ANDROID SOFTWARE DEVELOPMENT KIT

Head over to the Android Developers website at http://developer.android.com. You'll become intimately familiar with these pages as you work on this platform. Once on the site, find the section labeled SDK and download the offered files with reckless abandon. On Windows, it's best if you use the offered installer. For you Mac and Linux users, you'll get a zip file. Set the appropriate files to downloading and move on while they finish.

ECLIPSE

For versions of Eclipse newer than 3.5, Google recommends that you get the classic version of the IDE. Tap your way to www.eclipse.org/downloads and locate Eclipse Classic. (This chapter has screenshots from 3.6.1; the latest is, however, 3.7.1.) Make sure you get the right version for your system: 32-bit or 64-bit. Now get your twiddling thumbs ready and wait for the installer to come through. Assuming that you're not connecting through a telephone line that makes hissing noises, you should be finished in just a few minutes.

In the meantime, I'll entertain you with an opera about the nature of kittens . . . wait no, no I won't. You're welcome to browse ahead in the book while you download the required files.

JAVA

You'll need to download and install Java on your system (depending on how much development you've done before, you might already have it installed). I assume you were already comfortable with Java before diving into this book; I'm also going to assume you're comfortable installing the JDK yourself.

GETTING EVERYTHING INSTALLED

At this point, the process becomes a little more complicated and the herd of cats start to wander in different directions. Depending on which platform you're running, you may have to skip ahead from time to time. If the title doesn't look like it applies to your operating system (OS), skip ahead until you find one that does. Bear with me; you'll be working on your first application in no time.

> **NOTE:** For the duration of this book, I'm going to assume you'll be using the Eclipse IDE for the majority of your development. I'll try to include command-line methods as well as Eclipse screenshots for all important commands and tasks in case you're rocking the terminal with Vim or Emacs.

INSTALLING ECLIPSE

Installing Eclipse, for the most part, is as simple as decompressing the file you've downloaded and putting the application somewhere you'll remember. I recommend not launching Eclipse just yet. Wait until you've got the Android SDK squared away (see the next section). You may want to make sure that you've got the latest development tools in place.

INSTALLING THE ANDROID SDK

With Eclipse now in place, you're just a few steps away from running your own Android application. Find the section that applies to your operating system, and follow the steps therein.

INSTALLING THE SDK FOR MAC USERS

To install the SDK, simply unzip the compressed file you downloaded from the Android Developers site (developer.android.com). Although you can unpack this file anywhere, I recommend placing it in /Users/*yourUserName*/Documents/android_sdk/.

If you are a command-line person, you should put two directories on your path as follows:

1. Navigate to /User/*yourUserName*/.profile.

2. Assuming that you installed the SDK in the location I recommended, add the following code all on one line:

```
export PATH="$PATH"/Users/*yourUserName*/Documents/android_
sdk/tools"/Users/*yourUserName*/Documents/android_sdk/
platform-tools"
```

Now, when you open a new terminal, typing which android will return the path where you installed your shiny new Android SDK. Keep this command in mind—you'll return to it in a minute.

INSTALLING THE SDK FOR LINUX USERS

Linux users should go through nearly the same steps as in "Installing the SDK for Mac Users." The only differences are the instructions for putting the SDK on your path and where you may want to put your version of the SDK. I'm going to assume that if you're a Linux user, you're savvy enough to figure out this procedure on your own.

INSTALLING THE SDK FOR WINDOWS USERS

To install the Android SDK for Windows, follow these steps:

1. Start the Android SDK installer.

2. Accept the installer's default location and Start-menu configuration.

3. Let the installer work its magic.

   This procedure will add an SDK Manager command to your Start menu. This is the application you'll work with to select the correct platforms in the next section.

DOWNLOADING A PACKAGE

All right, you've got the SDK downloaded and in the right place. You're not quite there yet.

1. If you are a Mac or Linux user, run *sdk location*/tools/android; if you are a Windows user, allow the installer to open the AVD (Android Virtual Device) Manager software.

   You should see the Android SDK Manager.

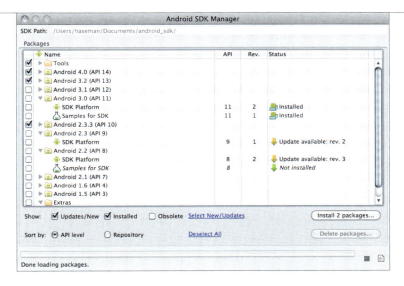

FIGURE 1.1 Use the Android SDK Manager to select as many versions as you would like to install.

NOTE: If you've closed it, you can find the SDK Manager program in your Start menu under Android SDK Tools.

2. Select Available Packages from the options in the left panel.

3. Select as many versions of the SDK as you like from the panel on the right. (At press time, there are still a few phones running 1.6.) At the very least, you'll probably want Gingerbread (2.3.3), which many phones are running. You'll need Honeycomb (for tablets) and Ice Cream Sandwich (the latest and greatest) for the last chapter of the book. If you're in a rush, just grab 2.3.3 for now (**Figure 1.1**).

4. In the resulting dialog, click Install x Packages, agree to Google's terms (read at your own risk), and away you go.

   The Android SDK Manager should download and install the two required platforms for you. So far, so good.

Keep in mind that the platform you're downloading corresponds to a particular version of the Android OS running on devices. Older phones may not support all the SDK calls that the latest phones might. As you learn about various SDK calls, I'll show you strategies for dealing with older devices.

CONFIGURING ECLIPSE

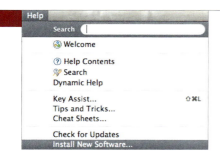

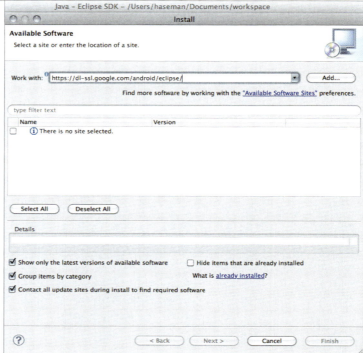

FIGURE 1.2 Where Eclipse has cleverly hidden the plug-in install wizard.

FIGURE 1.3 The plug-in install wizard in all its dull glory.

Fortunately, configuring Eclipse is consistent for Windows, Mac, and Linux. Fire up Eclipse and specify where you want to locate your workspace. It can, theoretically, be installed anywhere, but I always locate mine under `~/Documents/workspace` on my Mac. As long as you consistently use the same directory, you shouldn't encounter any problems.

ADDING THE ANDROID PLUG-IN TO ECLIPSE

Now that you've got Eclipse up and running, you'll need to add Android's ADT plug-in. This is the magic piece that will change Eclipse from a straight Java developer tool into a tool for making Android applications.

1. From the Eclipse Help menu, select Install New Software (**Figure 1.2**).

2. Enter **https://dl-ssl.google.com/android/eclipse/** in the Work With field in the Install pop-up. Your settings should look like those in **Figure 1.3**.

3. Give the site a name of your choosing. Mine was simply "android_stuff."

   You'll be presented with the option to install a few packages.

4. Select them all and click Next, then click Next again.

5. Accept Google's terms and conditions. Eclipse will download the appropriate plug-in packages.

> **NOTE:** If you're having trouble installing the Eclipse plug-ins, make sure you have an active Internet connection. Try using "http" instead of "https" for the plug-in URL. If all else fails, head over to http://developer.android.com/sdk/eclipse-adt.html#installing, where you'll find a few more helpful debugging steps.

   Before the download finishes, you might be warned that unsigned code is about to be installed. This is to be expected. (Don't freak out.)

6. Accept the unsigned code warning and allow the download to continue.

7. Restart Eclipse when prompted.

LOCATING THE SDK

One more step and you'll be able to create a project. You'll need to tell Eclipse where to find your Android SDK.

1. Start Eclipse. You should be staring at the helpful Welcome screen.

2. Choose File > Preferences.

   If everything you've done thus far is working, you should see an Android option in the list on the left.

3. Click Android.

FIGURE 1.4 Tell Eclipse where to find the Android SDK.

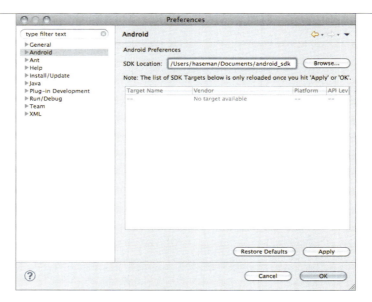

4. In the SDK Location field, enter the location to which you installed the SDK. **Figure 1.4** shows what it looks like on my Mac.

5. Click Apply.

In the large white box (which previously displayed "No target available"), you should now see a list of available SDK platforms.

If you're not seeing the list, then something isn't right. Head back to the "Downloading a Package" section and see what needs sorting out.

CREATING AN EMULATOR

Although I said you had only one more step before you could create a project, and that *is* true, you still need to create an emulator on which to run the project. So hang in, you're almost there.

1. With Eclipse running, click the icon on the top bar.

    Or, if you're a command-line junkie, run android in the shell (I'm going to assume you were able to add it to your path).

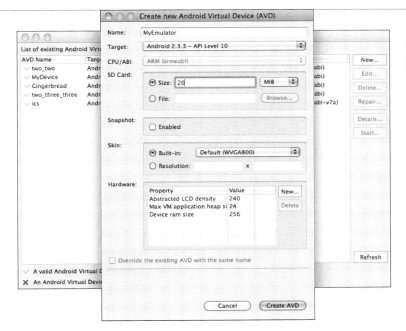

This screen should look familiar, because you just used it to install one or two application platforms. Now you're back to make a new virtual device.

2. With the Android SDK Manager open, make sure the Virtual Devices tab is selected and click New. A new emulator dialog will pop up.

3. In the Name field, give your emulator a name; it's best to give it one that helps distinguish it from any others. You will have collected several emulators before publishing your first application.

4. From the Target drop-down menu, specify which SDK you want to target. It's simplest right now to start with Gingerbread (2.3.3), but everything will still work on Ice Cream Sandwich (4.0).

5. In the SD Card field, select the Size radio button and enter a small size.

6. In the Skin section, select the Built-In radio button and choose Default WVGA800 from the drop-down menu.

The completed screen should look like **Figure 1.5**.

7. Click Create AVD and do a little dance next to your desk (or don't, it's up to you).

8. Select your new emulator and click the Start button to get it running. The laborious process of spinning up a new instance of the virtual device will begin.

NOTE: Pro emulator tip: Once you start an instance of the emulator, you don't ever have to start it up again. Reinstalling the application does not (as it does with many other systems) require you to spawn a new instance of the emulator.

WORKING WITH YOUR ANDROID PHONE

In almost all cases when I have an actual Android device, I'll do development on it over the emulator. One of the wonderful things about Android is how utterly simple it is to connect and work with nearly any Android phone. Here's what you'll need to do if you want to start working with your own device.

1. Find the USB cable that came with your phone, and plug it into your computer.

2. On your home screen, press the menu bar and go to Settings > Applications > Development and enable USB debugging by selecting the check box.

3. If you're on a Windows machine, you may need to install the general USB drivers. You can find them at http://developer.android.com/sdk/win-usb.html.

4. If you've finished everything correctly, you should see a little bug icon in the notification bar on your device. Your phone will work in exactly the same way an emulator would.

FIGURE 1.6 Your shiny new emulator.

Congratulations! If you've followed every step thus far, you have your very own shiny emulator or connected device, your Android SDK is correctly installed, and you're ready to rock and roll. Take a minute to bask in your own glory and play around with your new emulator (**Figure 1.6**) before moving on to the next section, which is about creating applications.

TIP: The emulator is a full Linux VM and can be a little heavy on the system resources (especially while Eclipse is running), so make sure your development machine has plenty of RAM.

CREATING A NEW
ANDROID PROJECT

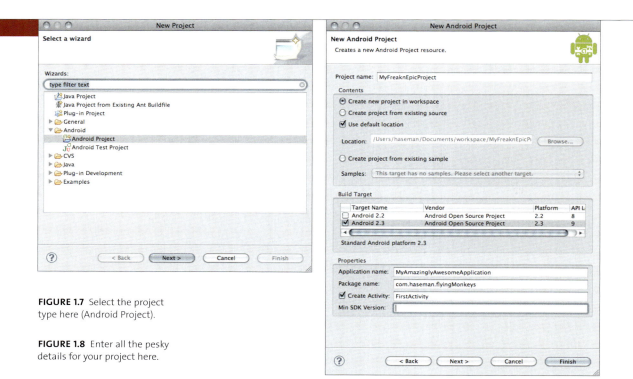

FIGURE 1.7 Select the project type here (Android Project).

FIGURE 1.8 Enter all the pesky details for your project here.

Google has provided a few helpful ways to create a new Android project.

1. Start Eclipse if it isn't already running.

2. Choose File > New > Project. You should see the New Project screen (**Figure 1.7**).

3. Click Next, and Android's friendly project creation wizard will start (**Figure 1.8**).

Let's go over what each field means to your project as you complete them.

NOTE: If you're not seeing the Android folder, you'll need to make sure you've correctly installed the Android Eclipse plug-in. Head back to "Configuring Eclipse" and see where things may have gone awry.

4. Enter a name for your project in the Project Name field.

   This is how Eclipse keeps track of your project. Further, it will create a folder with this name and put all your project files into it. The project name will not show up anywhere on the Android device once you install. The project name is something that really only matters to Eclipse, so I tend to pick descriptive names for projects.

5. In the Build Target section, select the version of Android you're targeting.

   Newer versions of Android always support applications built through older SDKs. They accomplish this with what's called *compatibility mode*. For now, try to target the most advanced version you can.

6. In the Application Name field, enter the full name of your application.

   This is what will show in the app drawer after you have installed your app.

7. In the Package Name field, enter the Java package where you will place your first activity.

8. Select the Create Activity check box and enter a name for your new activity in the text box.

   This step creates a new class with this name, so Java class naming conventions apply. In Chapter 2, you'll learn more specifics about what activities are and how they work.

9. Click Finish and you should be off to the races!

Now that you have a project, let's get it running.

CREATING A PROJECT FROM THE COMMAND LINE

If you prefer to work from the command line, you can simply enter the following three commands and move on with your day:

- ```
  android create project -n MyFantasticSimpleProject -t 9 -p
  myProjectDirectory -k com.haseman.fantasticProjctPackage -a
  NewActivity
  ```
- ```
  cd myProjectDirectory
  ```
- ```
  ant install
  ```

These commands create a new project and install a new application on an Android device. Assuming that you didn't run into any errors, you should find your sample app in the emulator's app drawer.
  ```

RUNNING A NEW PROJECT

Follow these steps to get your project running:

1. If your emulator isn't running, fire it back up. You need to make sure the IDE is in communication with the emulator; they frequently lose touch with each other. If you're using a device, make sure it's showing up correctly here as well.

2. Open the DDMS perspective by choosing Window > Open Perspective > Other.

   You should see a little android next to the DDMS option.

3. Open the DDMS perspective. Under the Devices tab, you should see an entry for your emulator or device.

4. From the Run menu in Eclipse, choose "Run last launched" or Run. Eclipse may ask you to confirm that the app is indeed an Android project.

   Android will compile, package, install, and run the application on your emulator or device. If you can see the app running on your phone, congrats! You've now officially created an Android application.

   > **TIP:** Command-line users can see DDMS by running...wait for it...ddms on the command line.

If you're sure your emulator is running, but it refuses to display in the list of devices, you may need to restart the Android Debug Bridge (ADB). Doing this requires getting into the terminal a little bit.

1. Open a terminal and change directories to the platform-tools folder inside your Android SDK folder. For me, the command looks like cd ~/Documents/android_sdk/platform-tools.

2. Run adb kill-server and count to 15.

3. Run adb start-server.

   When you run the start command, you should see the following lines:

   * daemon not running. starting it now on port 5037 *

   * daemon started successfully *

4. Switch back to your DDMS perspective; you should see the virtual device listed in the devices window.

5. Switch back to the Java perspective and, from the Run menu, select...wait for it...Run.

   It will ask you what kind of project it is.

6. Select Android. It may ask you which device you'd like to run your project on. Eclipse may also want to know which device you'd like to run your project on.

7. If your emulator isn't running, this will be your chance to start a new one. Otherwise, select your Android Virtual Device that is already running and click OK.

   Switching back to the emulator should show something close to **Figure 1.9**.

Although it doesn't do much, you've successfully created and run your first Android application. As Confucius said, a journey of a thousand miles begins with a single step.

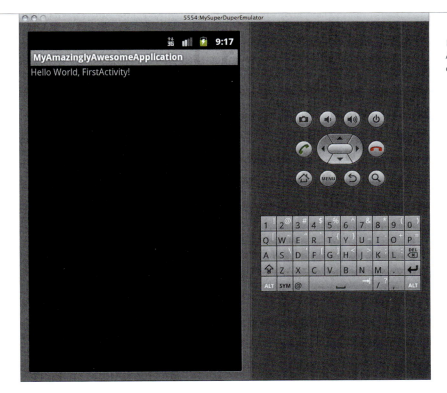

WRAPPING **UP**

This chapter covered downloading, installing, configuring, creating, and running Android applications. You now have the very basic tools that you'll need to continue with this book. Feel free, if you're struggling with the topics in the later chapters, to refer back to this chapter as needed.

THE **FILES**

Any mobile application, in its most basic form, consists of a single screen that launches by clicking an icon on the device's main screen.

When the SDK creates a basic Android project, it also creates several files and important directories.

As with any project, before you start building the structure it's important to at least take a quick look over the blueprints. Here are the file and folders that make up your Android project structure.

- AndroidManifest.xml

- /res

- /src

Throughout the rest of this chapter, I'll refer to the manifest and these folders.

THE MANIFEST

The AndroidManifest.xml file is your portal to the rest of the phone. In it, you'll describe which of your components should receive what events. You'll also declare, in the manifest file, what hardware and software your app will need permission to access. First, let's take a look at the <manifest> declaration in the AndroidManifest.xml file:

```
<manifest xmlns:android="http://schemas.android.com/apk/res/android"
    package="com.haseman.peachPit"
    android:versionCode="1"
    android:versionName="1.0">
```

There are a few noteworthy items in this code. The package definition tells Android in which Java package to look for the class files that make up the components of your application. The next two variables are not particularly important right now, but they will become vital once you're ready to ship your application to the Android Market. The versionCode is the number that helps the Market alert users that an update is available. The versionName is a string that the application menus and Market display to the user as the current version of your app.

Your application can have only one AndroidManifest.xml file. Henceforth, I'll refer to this file and concept simply as the manifest.

THE **ACTIVITY** CLASS

In a typical Android application, activities are the backbone of the operation. Essentially, their purpose is to control what is displayed on the screen. They bridge the gap between the data you wish to display and the UI layout files and classes that do the work of displaying the data. If you're familiar with the popular Model-View-Controller (MVC) architecture, the activity would be the control for a screen. Here's what the activity declaration looks like in the manifest file:

```
<activity android:name=".MyActivity"

    android:label="@string/app_name">
<!-- More on how the intent-filter works in the next section-->

    <intent-filter>

        <action android:name="android.intent.action.MAIN" />

        <category android:name="android.intent.category.LAUNCHER" />

    </intent-filter>

</activity>
```

The android:name tag tells the system what to place on the end of your package (from the manifest declaration) to find your class definition. For example, in my sample project at com.haseman.peachPit.MyActivity, the class loader will look to find a class that extends the Activity class.

In order to be found, the file must reside under the src/com/haseman/peachPit directory. This is standard operating procedure for the language that Android uses.

WATCHING THE ACTIVITY IN ACTION

The activity, if used correctly, is an object that specifically controls a single screen.

Let's talk about this mythical activity in terms of a real-world RSS news feed reader as a case study that can quickly explain what pages of theory would often miss. A developer typically uses one activity to list all feeds to which a user has subscribed. When a user taps a feed, the developer uses a second activity to display a list of available articles for that particular news feed. Lastly, when a user clicks a particular story, the developer uses a third activity to display article details.

It's easy to see how activities fill a certain role (subscription list, article list, article detail). At the same time, the activities are general, in that the article list should be able to display a list of articles from any RSS feed, and the article details activity should show the details from any article found through an RSS reader.

IMPLEMENTING YOUR OWN ACTIVITY

In most cases, the best way to understand something is to use it. With that in mind, let's add a new activity to the project you created in Chapter 1. This will explain how the activity works, its lifecycle, and what you need to know while working with it. Here are the general steps you'll need to follow:

1. Add an entry for the new activity into your manifest.

2. Create a new class that extends the Activity class.

3. Create a new file containing the XML layout instructions for this new activity, and add a new string literal for the layout to display (don't worry, this sounds a lot harder than it actually is).

4. When all the files are in place, you'll need to actually launch this new activity from your existing one.

THE MOST BASIC OF ACTIVITIES

In its simplest form, an activity is an object that extends the Activity class. It should, but doesn't have to, implement the onCreate method. Here's what your activity looks like by default when you create a new project:

```
public class MyActivity extends Activity {
    /** Called when the activity is first created. */
    @Override
    public void onCreate(Bundle savedInstanceState) {
        super.onCreate(savedInstanceState);
        setContentView(R.layout.main);
    }
}
```

In this code, the device calls the onCreate method as the activity is starting. onCreate tells the UI system that the setContentView method specifies the main layout file for this activity. Each activity may have one and only one content view, so once you set it, it can't be changed. This is how the Android SDK forces you to use a new activity for each screen, because each time you want to change your root content view, you'll need a different activity.

TELLING ANDROID ABOUT YOUR FRIENDLY NEW ACTIVITY

The Android system needs to know where to find your new activity when it comes time to load and launch it.

1. Open up the `AndroidManifest.xml` file in Eclipse.

2. Add the following line inside the `<application>` tag and directly after the `</activity>` closing tag of the previous declaration:

    ```
    <activity android:name=".NewActivity"/>
    ```

    This little line tells the system where to find the new activity in your application package. In the case of my demo, the class loader knows to look for the activity at `com.haseman.peachPit.NewActivity`.

Next, you'll need to put a file there for it to find.

CREATING THE NEWACTIVITY CLASS

There are several ways to create a new activity, but here is the easiest way to do it in Eclipse.

1. Right-click (or Control-click) the package name you've chosen (mine is `com.haseman.peachPit`).

2. Select New, then select Class.

3. Give the class a name in the dialog.

    A name is enough to create a new file. The file will be saved in your main package under the name you specified. In my demo, it is in my project under `src/com/haseman/peachPit/NewActivity.java`.

    Now that you have a class that extends an object, you'll need to switch it over to extend an activity.

4. Make the following highlighted change to your code:

```
package com.haseman.peachPit;
import android.app.Activity;
import android.os.Bundle;
public class NewActivity extends Activity{
    public void onCreate(Bundle icicle){
        super.onCreate(icicle);
    }
}
```

Notice that this code looks very similar to what is already in your existing activity. Let's make it a little bit different.

5. In the res/values/strings.xml file, add the following highlighted lines in the <resources> tag under the existing strings:

```
<resources>
    <!—other strings are omitted here for brevity-->
    <string name="new_activity_text">
        Welcome to the New Activity!
    </string>
</resources>
```

In these lines, you told Android that you want a new string with the name new_activity_text that can be accessed through Android's resource manager. You'll learn much more about the contents of the /values folder in later chapters. Next, you need to create a layout file for your new activity.

CREATING A NEW SCREEN LAYOUT

Here's how you create a new layout.

1. Create a new file named new_activity.xml inside the res/layout/ folder. It should sit next to the existing main.xml file (which is used by your existing activity). This new_activity.xml file should look almost exactly like main.xml, except you'll need to add a reference to the string you just created.

2. Insert the highlighted line to create a reference to the string you just created.

3. Give this modified TextView an ID so your Java code can reference it (you'll learn more about TextViews later; for now you should know that they're Android views that show text on the screen):

```xml
<?xml version="1.0" encoding="utf-8"?>

<LinearLayout xmlns:android="http://schemas.android.com/apk/
    res/android"
    android:orientation="vertical"
    android:layout_width="fill_parent"
    android:layout_height="fill_parent"

    >
<TextView
    android:id="@+id/new_activity_text_view"
    android:layout_width="fill_parent"
    android:layout_height="wrap_content"
    android:text="@string/new_activity_text"

    />
</LinearLayout>
```

I will devote Chapter 3 to resource management and user interface design, but for now just keep in mind that the @ prefix is how you tell Android you want to reference an ID, string, or drawable that is defined elsewhere as a resource.

Now that you have a new layout with its shiny new string, you'll need to tell the NewActivity class that you want it to use this particular layout file.

4. Add the following highlighted line to the onCreate method of your New Activity class:

```
public void onCreate(Bundle icicle){
    super.onCreate(icicle);
    setContentView(R.layout.new_activity);
}
```

setContentView is the method in which you tell Android which XML file to display for your new activity. Now that you've created a new class, string, and layout file, it's time to launch the activity and display your new view on the screen.

CATCHING KEYS

The simple way to launch your new activity is to have the user press the center key on his or her device. If your phone doesn't have a center key, you can easily modify the following code to accept any key you like. To listen for key events, you'll need to extend the original activity's onKeyDown method. Keep in mind that this is a simple example case. Launching a new activity when the user presses a single key probably isn't a very common use case in practice, but it makes for a good and simple example. Most new activities are started when a user selects a list item, presses a button, or takes another action with the screen.

Here's what your new version of onKeyDown should look like:

```
@Override
public boolean onKeyDown(int keyCode, KeyEvent event){
    if(keyCode == KeyEvent.KEYCODE_DPAD_CENTER){
        //Launch new Activity here!
        return true;
    }
    return super.onKeyDown(keyCode, event);
}
```

By declaring onKeyDown, you're overriding the default key handler in order to take action specific to your own activity. It's always a good idea to pass the incoming key to the parent class's version of the method if it's not something your activity handles on its own.

Notice that when the keyCode matches the center button, you return true. This is how you tell the Android activity and views that the key has been correctly handled and shouldn't be passed on to anyone else. Otherwise, you allow the activity superclass to handle the key. This may not seem like a big deal now, but it will become much more important as your Android activities become more complex.

LAUNCHING THE ACTIVITY

Finally, it's time to launch the new activity. This will start your brief foray into intents. Each new activity is started as the result of a new intent being dispatched into the system (which processes it and takes the appropriate action). In order to start the first activity, you'll need a reference of your application context and the class object for your new activity. Let's create the new intent first.

1. Place the following code into your onKeyDown key handling method:

    ```
    Intent startIntent=new Intent(
        this.getApplicationContext(),
        NewActivity.class);
    ```

    You're passing the new intent an application context and the class object of the activity that you would like to launch. This tells Android exactly where to look in the application package. There are many ways to create and interact with intents; this is, however, the simplest way to start up a new activity. Once the intent is properly constructed, it's simply a matter of telling the Android system that you'd like to start the new activity.

2. Put the following line into your key handling method:

    ```
    startActivity(startIntent);
    ```

FIGURE 2.1 Here is your new activity!

Your onKeyDown handler should look like the following:

```
public boolean onKeyDown(int keyCode, KeyEvent event){
    if(keyCode == KeyEvent.KEYCODE_DPAD_CENTER){
        Intent startIntent=new Intent(this, NewActivity.class);
        startActivity(startIntent);
        return true;
    }
    return super.onKeyDown(keyCode, event);
}
```

NOTE: Throughout this whole process, the original activity has never once had access to the instance of the new activity. Any information that might pass between these two activities must go through the intermediary intent. You'll learn how this is done in the next section.

TRYING IT OUT

If you're running Eclipse and you've been coding along with me, it should now be a simple matter of spinning up the emulator and installing your new activity (the steps for which you should remember from Chapter 1). Once your new application has launched, press the center key to see the results of all your labor (**Figure 2.1**).

Now that you know how to create and launch a new activity, it's time to discuss how that process works. You'll need to understand, for the purposes of UI layout and data management/retention later, what methods are called each time one of your activities makes its way onto, and off of, the screen.

Intents can take a myriad of forms.

You use them anytime you need to start an activity or service. Further, you'll frequently use intents for system-wide communication. For example, you can receive notifications about power system changes by registering for a widely published intent. If one of your activities registers for an intent in the manifest (for example, com.haseman.peachPit.OhOhPickMe), then any application anywhere on the phone can, if you make your activity public, launch directly to your activity by calling

```
startActivity(new Intent("com.haseman.peachPit.OhOhPickMe"));
```

THE LIFE AND TIMES OF AN ACTIVITY

It's good to know early on that each activity lives a very short but exciting life. It begins when an intent that your activity is registered to receive is broadcast to the system. The system calls your activity's constructor (while also starting your application as necessary) before invoking the following methods on the activity, in this order:

1. onCreate

2. onStart

3. onResume

When you implement an activity, it's your job to extend the methods that make up this lifecycle. The only one you are required to extend is onCreate. The others, if you declare them, will be called in the lifecycle order.

Your activity is the top visible application, can draw to the screen, will receive key events, and is generally the life of the party. When the user presses the Back key from the activity, these corresponding methods are called in the following order:

1. onPause

2. onStop

3. onDestroy

After these methods have executed, your activity is closed down and should be ready for garbage collection.

In order to make sense of the activity's flow, let's quickly look over each lifecycle method in detail. Remember that you must evoke the superclass call in each of these methods (often before you do anything else) or Android will throw exceptions at you.

NOTE: onCreate is the only one of the application lifecycle methods that you must implement. I've found, in most of my work with Android, that I only end up implementing one or two of these methods depending on what each activity is responsible for.

PUBLIC VOID ONCREATE(BUNDLE ICICLE)

Android will call your declaration of this method as your activity is starting. Remember, however, that during the run of your application you may go through several instances of each activity. If, for example, the user changes the screen orientation from landscape to portrait, your activity will be destroyed and a new instance of the same activity will be created and initialized.

If the title, say, for your activity is dynamic but will not change after the activity is started, this method would be where you'd want to reach into the view hierarchy and set up the title. This method is not the place to configure data that could change while the app is in the background or when another activity is launched on top of it.

Further, if your app is running in the background and the system is running low on resources, your application may be killed. If that happens, the onCreate method will be called on a new instance of the same activity when your application returns to the foreground.

The onCreate method is also your one and only chance to call setContentView for your activity. This, as you saw earlier, is how you tell the system what layout you'd like to use for this screen. You call setContentView once you can begin setting data on the UI. This could be anything from setting the contents of lists to TextViews or ImageViews.

PUBLIC VOID ONSTART()

When starting up, your onStart method is called immediately after onCreate. If your app was put in the background (either by another application launching over yours or the user pressing the Home button), onStart will be called as you resume but before the activity can interact with the screen. I tend to avoid overriding onStart unless there's something specific I need to check when my application is about to begin using the screen.

PUBLIC VOID ONRESUME()

onResume is the last method called in the activity lifecycle as your activity is allowed access to the screen. If UI elements have changed while your activity was in the background, this method is the place to make sure the UI and phone state are in sync.

When your activity is starting up, this method is called after onCreate and onStart. When your activity is coming to the foreground again, reguardless of what state it was in before, onResume will be called.

HOORAY, YOUR ACTIVITY IS NOW RUNNING!

After all this setup, configuration, and work, your activity is now visible to the user. Things are being clicked, data may be parsed and displayed, lists are scrolled, and things are happening! At some point, however, the party must end (perhaps because the user pressed the Back key) and you'll need to wind things down.

ONPAUSE()

onPause is the first method called by the system as your application is leaving the screen. If you have any processes or loops (animations, for example) that should be running only while your activity is onscreen, the onPause method is the perfect place to stop them. onPause will be called on your activity if you've launched another activity over the one you're currently displaying.

Keep in mind that if the system needs resources, your process could be killed anytime after the onPause method is called. This isn't a normal occurrence, but you need to be aware that it could happen.

The onPause method is important because it may be the only warning you get that your activity (or even your entire application stack) is going away. It is in this method that you should save any important information to disk, your database, or the preferences.

Once your activity has actually left the screen, you'll receive the next call in the activity lifecycle.

ONSTOP()

When Android calls your onStop method, it indicates that your activity has officially left the screen. Further, onStop is called when the user is leaving your activity to interact with another one. This doesn't necessarily mean that your activity is shutting down (although it could). You can only assume that the user has left your activity for another one. If you're doing any ongoing process from within your activity that should run only while it's active, this method is your chance to be a good citizen and shut it down.

ONDESTROY()

onDestroy is your last method call before oblivion. This is your last chance for your activity to clean up its affairs before it passes on to the great garbage collector in the sky.

Any background processes that your activity may have been running in the background (fetching/parsing data, for example) must be shut down on this method call.

However, just because onDestroy is called doesn't mean that your activity will be obliterated. So if you have a thread running, it may continue to run and take up system resources even after the onDestroy method is called.

BONUS ROUND—DATA RETENTION METHODS

As mentioned earlier, your process can be killed at any point after onPause if the system needs resources. The user, however, shouldn't ever know that this culling has occurred. In order to accomplish this, Android gives you two chances to save your state data for later use.

ONSAVEINSTANCESTATE(BUNDLE OUTSTATE)

This method passes you a bundle object into which you can put any data that you'd need to restore your activity to its current state at a later time. You'll do this by calling something like outState.putString or outState.putBoolean. Each stored value requires a string key going in, and it requires the same string key to come back out. You are responsible for overriding your own onSaveInstanceState method. If you've declared it, the system will call it; otherwise, you've missed your chance.

When your previously killed activity is restored, the system will call your onCreate method again and hand back to you the bundle you built with onSaveInstanceState.

onSaveInstanceState will only be called if the system thinks you may have to restore your activity later. It wouldn't be called if, for example, the user has pressed the Back key, as the device clearly has no need to resume this exact activity later. As such, this method is not the place for saving user data. Only stash temporary information that is important to the UI on this particular instance of the screen.

ONRETAINNONCONFIGURATIONINSTANCE()

When the user switches between portrait and landscape mode, your activity is destroyed and a new instance of it is created (going through the full shutdown-startup cycle of method calls). When your activity is destroyed and created specifically because of a configuration change (the device rotation being the most common), onRetainNonConfigurationInstance gives you a chance to return any object that can be reclaimed in your new activity instance by calling getLastNonConfigurationInstance.

This tactic helps to make screen rotation transitions faster. Keep this in mind if it takes your activity a significant amount of time to acquire data that it plans on displaying to the screen. Instead, you can get the previously displayed data by using getLastNonConfigurationInstance.

KEEP IT SIMPLE, SMARTY

By now you know that activities can be killed off with very little notice. The onSaveInstanceState gives you a chance to save primitives for later use. This means, unequivocally, that your entire activity must be able to collapse all its important information into a series of primitives. This further reinforces the notion that activities must be very simple and *cannot* contain any complex data important to the application outside itself. Avoid keeping large Java collections filled with data in your activity, as it may be terminated with very little notice.

You should now have a basic understanding of

- Steps for creating a new activity
- How an activity is started
- The lifecycle of an activity

You have what you need to keep up as I go over more complex topics in later chapters. Fear not, I'll come back to the activity in no time.

THE **INTENT** CLASS

An intent is a class. Intents, in the Android platform, make up the major communication protocol for moving information between application components. In a well-designed Android application, components (activity, content provider, or service) should never directly access an instance of any other component. As such, intents are how these pieces are able to communicate.

A good half of this book could be dedicated to the creation, use, and details of the Intent class. For the sake of brevity and getting you up and running as fast as possible, I'll cover only a few basics in this chapter. Look for intents throughout the rest of this book. They're probably the most often used class in Android as a whole.

There are two main ways to tell the Android system that you'd like to receive intents sent out by the system, by other applications, or even by your own app:

- Registering an <intent-filter> in the AndroidManifest.xml file
- Registering an IntentFilter object at runtime with the system

In each case, you need to tell the Android system what events you want to listen for.

There are huge heaping numbers of ways to send intents as well. You can broadcast them out to the system as a whole, or you can target them to a specific activity or service. However, in order to start a service or activity, it must be registered in the manifest (you saw an example of this in the previous demonstration on starting a new activity).

Let's take a look at how to use intents in practice.

MANIFEST REGISTRATION

Why not register everything at runtime? If an intent is declared as part of your manifest, the system will start your component so that it will receive it. Registration at runtime presupposes that you are already running. For this reason, anytime you want your application to awaken and take action based on an event, declare it in your manifest. If it's something your application should receive only while it's running, register an IntentFilter (it's an intent-filter when declared in XML, but an IntentFilter in your Java code) once your particular component has started.

Let's go back to the initial application and look again at the activity's entry in the manifest:

```
<activity android:name=".MyActivity"
    android:label="@string/app_name">
    <intent-filter>
        <action android:name="android.intent.action.MAIN" />
        <category android:name="android.intent.category.LAUNCHER" />
    </intent-filter>
</activity>
```

The android.intent.action.MAIN declaration tells the system that this activity is the main activity for your application. No parameters are needed to start it. It's a good idea to list only one activity as MAIN in the manifest. This is also how adb (the Android debug bridge), when you run your application from Eclipse, knows which activity to start up.

The android.intent.category.LAUNCHER category tells the system that the enclosing activity should be launched when your icon is clicked on the main phone's application dock. Further, it tells Android that you'd like the icon to appear in the app launcher drawer. This is an example of an intent-filter that's created for you by Android's project creation tools. Let's add one of our own.

ADDING AN INTENT

If you skipped the previous section about the Activity class, now may be a good time to go back and at least skim over the code. In that section, I showed you how to declare and launch a simple new activity. What I didn't show you, however, was how to make that activity accessible to the system as a whole by declaring an <intent-filter> for it within your manifest. Let's do that now.

1. Add an intent-filter to the NewActivity declaration:

```
<activity android:name=".NewActivity">
    <intent-filter>
        <action android:name="com.haseman.PURPLE_PONY_POWER"/>
```

```
        <category android:name="android.intent.category.
         ↪ DEFAULT"/>
    </intent-filter>
</activity>
```

In this code, you've registered for intents containing the `com.haseman.PURPLE_PONY_POWER` action and set the `intent-filter` category to default.

Now, lest you think I'm a crazed children's toy enthusiast, I've used this rather absurdist action string to demonstrate a point—namely, that the only requirement for the action string is that it be unique for your particular component.

In the previous section, I showed you how to launch the new activity by using the following lines:

```
Intent startIntent=new Intent(this, NewActivity.class);

startActivity(startIntent);
```

This works, but it has one major limitation: It cannot be launched outside your own application's context. This renders useless one of the most powerful features that the activity-intent model has to offer. Namely, any application on the device, with the right intent, can use components within your application.

Now that you've added the `<intent-filter>` to the sample project manifest, you can launch this particular activity anywhere with the following code:

```
Intent actionStartIntent= new Intent
 ↪ ("com.haseman.PURPLE_PONY_POWER");

startActivity(actionStartIntent);
```

Notice a very important difference between this code and the listing above it. When you create the intent in this example, you're not required to pass in a `Context` object (the bundle of information that is required to communicate with the system at large). This allows any application, with knowledge of the required intents, to start the `NewActivity` class.

2. Add the highlighted code to the onKeyDown handler to launch the same activity in a different way. Here's how the new OnKeyDown method should look:

```
public boolean onKeyDown(int keyCode, KeyEvent event){
    if(keyCode == KeyEvent.KEYCODE_DPAD_CENTER){
        Intent startIntent=new Intent(this,
        → NewActivity.class);
        startActivity(startIntent);
        return true;
    }
    if(keyCode == KeyEvent.KEYCODE_DPAD_DOWN){
        Intent actionStartIntent=
            new Intent("com.haseman.PURPLE_PONY_POWER");
        startActivity(actionStartIntent);
    }
    return super.onKeyDown(keyCode, event);
}
```

Now, when you press the down key in the sample application, you'll see the same activity launching using this new manifest-declared intent-filter.

If you've misspelled the intent's action string or neglected to add the default category to your intent-filter, you may get an android.content.Activity NotFoundException.

This exception will be thrown by the startActivity method anytime you create an intent that the system cannot connect to an activity listed in a manifest on the device.

Registering for intent filters is not only the purview of the activity. Any Android application component can register to be started when an intent action is broadcast by the system.

One activity may register to receive any number of events. Typically, sending an intent is akin to telling the activity "do this one thing!" That "one thing" can be anything from editing a file to displaying a list of possible files or actions. Again, as we've discussed, it's important to limit the scope of your activity, so registering for only one intent is often a good idea. However, because your activity could be registered for more than one intent, it's a good idea to call getIntent inside your onCreate method and check why you're being started so you can take the right action (by calling getAction).

LISTENING FOR INTENTS AT RUNTIME

Another method for receiving events that pertain only to your application or for receiving events broadcast by the Android system itself is to listen for the intents at runtime.

Let's say that your activity would like to show a special screen or take a custom action when the user enables Airplane mode. To do this, you'll need to create a temporary IntentFilter and an inner BroadcastReceiver object instance.

CREATE A RECEIVER

Let's add the runtime BroadcastReceiver to the MyActivity class. A Broadcast Receiver is, as you can probably guess, an object with a single onReceive method.

Change the MyActivity class to look like the following:

```
public class MyActivity extends Activity {
    private BroadcastReceiver simpleReceiver=new BroadcastReceiver() {
        public void onReceive(Context context, Intent intent) {
            if(intent.getAction().equals(
                Intent.ACTION_AIRPLANE_MODE_CHANGED)){
                    Toast.makeText(context,
                    R.string.airplane_change,
                    Toast.LENGTH_LONG).show();
            }
        }
    };
//Rest of the Activity is here.
}
```

FIGURE 2.2 Do you want to
open that YouTube link in the
browser or the app?

CREATING SELF-CONTAINED BROADCAST RECEIVERS

A broadcast receiver doesn't have to exist inside an activity. You can register a
receiver if you want to know about a system event but might not need to start your
full application when it occurs.

BroadcastReceivers can be registered on their own under the `<receiver>` tag.
In practice, I use these as a way to receive information about the system that may
not require showing something to the user. Starting an activity only to shut it down
if it's not needed is much more resource expensive than grabbing the broadcast
intent with a receiver and then starting up an activity only when needed.

HANDLING COLLIDING ACTIVITIES

You may be thinking to yourself "Self, what happens when more than one activity is registered for the same intent?" This is a very interesting question, one that
Android resolves simply by asking the user.

If two activities listen for the same intent in their manifests, and an application
attempts to start an activity with that intent, the system will pop up a menu giving
users a list of possible applications to choose from (**Figure 2.2**).

You've probably seen similar behavior hundreds of times on your desktop computer, such as when opening a file and being given a choice about which application
you'd like to open it with.

FIGURE 2.3 What happens when you share my funny-looking Android avatar?

This notion of many activities registering for the same intent can have delightful side effects. In Android, any application can register to share media with a given MIME time by using the `android.intent.action.SEND` action.

Figure 2.3 is what the Share tab on my phone looks like when I press it in the image gallery.

It is this ability to register for similar intents that allows seamless interaction as each application registering this intent is given an entry on the Share menu. Clicking an entry in this list will start the registered activity and pass along as an extra the location at which the image can be accessed. What is an extra? Good question.

MOVING YOUR OWN DATA

One of the major features of the intent is the ability to package and send data along with it. One activity should never directly manipulate the memory of another. However, they still must have a way to communicate information. This communication is accomplished with the help of the intent's `Extra` bundle. The bundle can hold any number of string-primitive pairs. Perhaps the best way to illustrate this concept is with some code and an example.

Earlier, I showed you how to start a new activity by using an action-based broadcast intent.

Add the following highlighted code to the onKeyDown listener that you've dealt with before:

```
public boolean onKeyDown(int keyCode, KeyEvent event){
//...previous keycode code skipped...
if(keyCode == KeyEvent.KEYCODE_DPAD_DOWN){
    Intent actionStartIntent= new Intent("com.haseman.
    → PURPLE_PONY_POWER");
    actionStartIntent.putExtra("newBodyText",
"You Pressed the Down Key!");
    startActivity(actionStartIntent);
}
```

You're adding a string payload to the intent before using it to start an activity. Whoever receives the intent will be able to pull this string out (assuming they know it's there) and use it as they see fit. Now that you know how to attach the data, let's take a look at an example of retrieving and using the string in NewActivity's onCreate method:

```
public void onCreate(Bundle icicle){
    super.onCreate(icicle);
    setContentView(R.layout.new_activity);
    Intent currentIntent = getIntent();
    if(currentIntent.hasExtra("newBodyText")){
        String newText = currentIntent.getExtras().
        → getString("newBodyText");
        TextView bodyView = (TextView)findViewById(
            R.id.new_activity_text_view);
        bodyView.setText(newText);
    }
```

In the highlighted code, I'm getting the intent that was responsible for starting my `NewActivity` by calling `getIntent`. Next, I'm checking if this intent actually contains the `newBodyText` extra. Keep in mind that the intent may not contain the extra. If you forget to check for this case, you'll quickly find yourself inundated with `NullPointerExceptions`. If the extra is there, I'll pull it out and set the string as the new text in my display. The last two lines obtain a reference to the screen's text view and change the text to be the contents of the extra. Don't worry about the mechanics of that particular operation right now; you'll learn more about this topic in depth later.

REVIEWING INTENTS

You've learned how to register for, create, and use the basic functionality of an intent. As you now know, they can be registered for in the manifest or at runtime. They can be sent by any application on the phone, and any number of application components can register for the same intent.

The goal in this section was to get you started on the care and feeding of Android intents. In future chapters and tasks, you'll work with intents again in many different contexts.

THE **APPLICATION** CLASS

Typically, an Android application is a collection of activities, broadcast receivers, services, and content providers. The Application class is the glue that binds all these disparate pieces into a singular, unified entity. Every time a content provider, activity, service, or intent receiver in your manifest is initialized, an Application class is also spun up and available to it.

THE DEFAULT APPLICATION DECLARATION

Looking in the AndroidManifest.xml file, you'll see a typical Application declaration that looks like the following:

```
<application android:icon="@drawable/icon"
    android:label="@string/app_name">
<!--Activities, Services, Broadcast Receivers, and Content Providers -->
</application>
```

Here you can see the <application> tag. This part of the manifest typically contains information relevant to your application at large. android:icon tells the system what icon to display in the main application list. android:label in this case refers to another entry in the strings.xml file you were editing earlier.

CUSTOMIZING YOUR OWN APPLICATION

Adding your own application is very similar to the steps you've already gone through to add a new activity.

1. Add a name field to the existing AndroidManifest.xml declaration.

2. Create a new class in your package that extends the Application class.

3. Profit!

Let's go over steps 1 and 2 in depth. You're on your own for step 3.

THE NAME

When it comes to the manifest, android:name refers not to the name of the object being described, but to the location of the class in your Java package. The Application declaration is no exception. Here's what the opening tag of the application should look like with the new declaration:

```
<application android:icon="@drawable/icon"
    android:label="@string/app_name"
    android:name= ".SampleApplication">
```

In this declaration, you tell the system what icon you want to represent your application on the Android application drawer.

Once again, the class loader will look for your Application class by appending the contents of android:name to the end of your package declaration within the <manifest> opening tag. Now you'll need to actually create this class to keep the class loader from getting unhappy.

THE APPLICATION CLASS

Here's what you'll need, at a very basic level, to have an Application of your very own:

```
import android.app.Application;
public class SampleApplication extends Application{
    public void onCreate(){
        super.onCreate();
    }
}
```

The Application can be a very simple class. It's hard to understand what the Application can do for you until you consider a few things:

- Activities are very transient.

- Activities have no access to each other's memory, and they should communicate through intents.

- As activities are constantly being stopped and started for a variety of reasons, there's no way for your activity to know if it's being started for the very first time in the run of your application. The Application class's onCreate method, on the other hand, is called only when your app is being initialized. As such, it can be a good place to take actions that should happen only when your application is first started.

If you need a temporary holding pen for data that may span many activities, a data member that's part of the Application can be a convenient place to store it. You must be very careful about adding data to the Application. Any single component declared in your manifest, from the simplest BroadcastReceiver to the most complex activity, will, before it's created by the system, first create your Application object. This means you must make the Application's onCreate method run as fast as you possibly can.

ACCESSING THE APPLICATION

All your broadcast receivers, services, activities, and content providers have a method called getApplication provided to them by the appropriate superclass. When invoked, getApplication will return a pointer to your Application object if you specified one in the manifest. Getting access to it, now that you've declared and created the class, is as simple as calling getApplication and casting the returned object to an instance of your own pointer. Here's what it looks like:

```
SampleApplication myApplication = (SampleApplication)
getApplication();
```

That's all there is to it. You can add public data members or context-sensitive methods to your own version of the Application, and with one call all your components will have access to the same object, like so:

```
public class SampleApplication extends Application{
    public String username;
    public void onCreate(){
        super.onCreate();
    }
}
```

To access your newly added variable, simply do the object cast listed earlier:

```
public void onCreate(Bundle bundle){
    SampleApplication myApplication =
        (SampleApplication)getApplication();
    myApplication.username = "sparks";
}
```

Be sure that any data you put in the Application is relevant everywhere, because the overhead for allocating and initializing the Application can become a drag on startup times.

WRAPPING UP

Over the course of this chapter, I've exposed you to the fundamental building blocks of an Android application. I used examples to get you started on

- The manifest

- Creating and using your own activities

- Sending, receiving, and taking advantage of intents

- Creating your own Application object

It's my hope that through the rest of the book, you'll be able to use the building blocks you've learned in this chapter to understand how an Android application functions. From here on out, I'll be focusing more on how to do tasks rather than on the theories that back them. On that note, let's start making screens that include more than just a single text view.

THE **VIEW** CLASS

No, this isn't a television show where several women debate the merits of common culture. The View class is the superclass for all the Android display objects. Each and every user interface (UI) class from the simple ImageView to the mighty RelativeLayout all subclass from this same object. In this section, you'll learn the basics of creating, adding, and modifying your existing layouts using Java code and XML. You'll also learn to create your own custom view. A view, at its very core, is simply a rectangle into which you can display something. Subclasses take many different forms, but they all need, simply, a space to show something to the user.

CREATING A VIEW

Creating a new view is something you've already done. In Chapter 1, you added a view to an XML layout file as part of exploring how to launch a new activity. At the time, I told you we'd get into the specifics of how these views were created and modified, and, well, now's the time! Let's take a look at the default views generated for you automatically when you create a new Android project.

VIEWS IN XML

Here's what the default XML layout looks like in a new project:

```xml
<?xml version="1.0" encoding="utf-8"?>

<LinearLayout xmlns:android="http://schemas.android.com/apk/res/
  android"

    android:orientation="vertical"

    android:layout_width="fill_parent"

    android:layout_height="fill_parent"

    >

<TextView

    android:layout_width="fill_parent"

    android:layout_height="wrap_content"

    android:text="@string/hello"

    />

</LinearLayout>
```

For now, it's important to note that every single layout *must* have a value set for both its height and its width. Android may not fail to compile if you do not specify these values (as they could be updated at runtime), but if it starts to draw your views and the system height and width values are missing, then your application will crash.

Question: Which of the two elements (LinearLayout and TextView) in this default XML layout are views?

Answer: Both.

All visual objects onscreen subclass from the View class. If you go high enough in the inheritance chain, you'll find an "extends View" somewhere.

In the default XML layout, the Android tools have added a simple TextView contained inside a LinearLayout. When displayed onscreen, the contents of the hello string will appear by default in the upper-left corner of the screen. I'll discuss how to position visual elements onscreen later in this chapter.

To display the XML layout onscreen, you need to call the setContentView() method and pass the name of the layout to the activity.

In Eclipse, your code editor, it should look like this:

```
@Override
public void onCreate(Bundle savedInstanceState) {
    super.onCreate(savedInstanceState);
    setContentView(R.layout.main);
}
```

In this code, you're telling the activity that you want it to inflate and render the main layout for this activity. By inflating, I mean the conversion from the XML in the project to a Java object that can be told to draw on the screen. You might be thinking, "Is it possible to build and display a layout and view within Java alone? Can I skip layout in XML entirely and go straight to the source?" Yes, you can, but in practice you shouldn't. Even so, understanding how to build a layout without the XML will help you potentially modify any aspect of your layout at runtime.

VIEWS IN JAVA

Anything you can lay out or build in XML, you can lay out and build also within the Java code itself; it's just more complex. It's important, however, to understand what Android is doing as it inflates and builds your layouts.

Here's what the Java code looks like to build the exact same user interface that Android generates for you in XML when you create a new project:

```java
public void onCreate(Bundle savedInstanceState) {
    super.onCreate(savedInstanceState);
    setContentView(buildLayouts());
}
public View buildLayouts(){
    LinearLayout topView =
        new LinearLayout(getApplicationContext());
LayoutParams topLayoutParams =
        new FrameLayout.LayoutParams
        (LayoutParams.MATCH_PARENT,
        LayoutParams.MATCH_PARENT);
    topView.setLayoutParams(topLayoutParams);
    TextView textView =
new TextView(getApplicationContext());
    LinearLayout.LayoutParams textLayoutParams =
            new LinearLayout.LayoutParams(
            LayoutParams.WRAP_CONTENT,
            LayoutParams.MATCH_PARENT);
    textView.setLayoutParams(textLayoutParams);
    textView.setText(R.string.hello);
    topView.addView(textView);
    return topView;
}
```

SPECIAL **DIMENSIONS**

You are always required to give a height and width for every view in your hierarchy. You may use, for these definitions in particular, four different values. They are:

- `wrap_content` makes the view big enough to match what it contains. This might mean different things to different views, but the concept remains the same.

- `fill_parent` and `match_parent` values actually mean exactly the same thing. Namely, I want the dimensions of this view to match the dimensions of my parent view.

- `dip` or `dp` stands for device-independent pixels. This is a value that will give you a consistent spacing regardless of the screen density (pixels per inch) of the device. On the Nexus 1 or Nexus S, 1 dp ~= 1.5 pixels.

- px stands for pixels. There are times when exact pixel values are necessary. I advise against using this to declare screen locations, but it's an option.

Let's look at what is happening in the Java code. Instead of calling `setContentView` on an ID from the `R.java` file, I'm passing it an instance that the `LinearLayout` object returned from the `buildLayouts` method. In the `buildLayouts` method, I'm first creating a new `LinearLayout` (passing in the application's context) and a new `LayoutParams` object. To match what's in the XML, the new `LayoutParam` is initialized with both the `width` and the `height` set to `MATCH_PARENT`. If you have done Android development before, you should know that `MATCH_PARENT` is exactly the same as the previously used `FILL_PARENT`.

Once I have the layout parameters initialized for the top `LinearLayout`, I can pass them to the object with a `setLayoutParams` call. I've now got the `LinearLayout` configured, so it's time to move on to building the `TextView`.

This is a simple text view, so its layout parameters are very similar to those of its parent's layout. The only noticeable difference is that I'm setting the height, when creating the layout parameters, to scale to fit the natural size of the `TextView`. (Much more on dynamic heights and widths soon.)

Once I've told the `TextView` how it will be positioned in its parent layout via the layout parameters, I tell it which string I'd like to display. This string is defined in `/res/values/strings.xml`. The name attribute in XML determines what needs to appear after `R.string` for the system to locate your resource. You'll learn much more about resource management in the next section.

Last, I need to add the new `TextView` into the `LinearLayout` and then return the `LinearLayout` so it can be set as the main content view for the activity. Once that's finished, I have a layout constructed at runtime with Java code, which identically matches the layout provided by the system in XML form.

The Java code looks fairly straightforward, but XML is a much better idea for working with the layout. Using XML, you can use Android's resource management system and give non-software engineers the ability to modify the application UI.

ALTERING THE UI AT RUNTIME

It's one thing to use XML or Java to define the pile of views that compose your user interface. But particularly in the XML case, you'll want to be able to retrieve and alter views with data acquired over the network, from the user, or from any other information source. Android provides a simple method for gaining access to the views that currently compose your screens by calling `findViewById`, which is an `Activity` class method.

IDENTIFYING YOUR VIEWS

Before you can find one of your views at runtime, you'll need to give it an ID. Once you've called `setContentView` on an activity, you can call `findViewById` to retrieve your views and then alter them. This process should look at least a little bit familiar, because you saw it in the previous chapter. Here's what it looks like in XML:

```
<TextView
    android:id="@+id/text_holder"
    android:layout_width="fill_parent"
    android:layout_height="wrap_content"
    android:text="@string/hello"
    />
```

In this case, I've added an `android:id` line to name the `TextView`. The `@+` notation tells Android that rather than referring to a view, you'd like to create an ID for the view. The first reference to any ID must start with `@+id`. Subsequent references to that ID will start simply with `@id`.

Android keeps its own reserved IDs name-space. For example, if you're creating a layout to be used by `ListActivity` (an activity specifically designed to show lists of information), you'll want to set the ID on your main onscreen `ListView` to `"android:id="@id/android:list"`. These well-known IDs allow Android's system code to correctly find and interact with the list view that you specify. I'll provide you with more on this subject in Chapter 5, which covers list creation and management.

If you're creating a view at runtime, simply call `setId` and pass in an integer, and you'll be able to retrieve it later.

FINDING YOUR RESOURCES WITH ANDROID

When Android compiles your project, it assigns a number value for your new static numeric ID. It places this new ID in the `R.java` file within your project. This file is your gateway to everything you've defined inside the `res` folder. For every layout, drawable, and identified view—and for a host of other things—Android places a subsequent statically defined `int` into the R file that identifies those things. Anytime you add a line to your layout XML defining a new ID (for example, `android:id="@+id/my_new_id"`), you'll find that after the next time you compile your project, you'll have an entry in the `R.id` class. In the previous example, this entry would be `R.id.my_new_id`.

RETRIEVING A VIEW

Getting the existing instance of an Android view is as simple as calling `findViewById` and passing in the ID value found in the `R.java` file. Given the earlier XML example, here's how you would grab an instance of the text view and modify its contents.

```
public void onCreate(Bundle savedInstanceState) {
        super.onCreate(savedInstanceState);
        setContentView(R.layout.main);
    TextView tv = (TextView)findViewById(R.id.text_holder);
    if(tv!=null)
        tv.setText(R.string.hello);
}
```

If you are reading this book in order, this should look eerily familiar. I'm retrieving an instance of the text view as described by the layout XML. Remember that calling findViewById only works after you've called setContentView within the onCreate method. Also, it's always a good idea to check for null to make sure the system was able to retrieve what you're looking for. Later layouts for different screen configurations may not have all the views your current layout does. Think of it as future-proofing your UI code for different landscape layouts.

KEEPING YOUR VIEWS AROUND

Calling findViewById will return an object that persists for the duration of your activity. This means you can add private data members to your Activity class to reduce the number of times you need to reach into the view hierarchy and find them. If you modify a view only once or twice during the lifetime of your activity, this trick won't save you much time, but it can save significant time if you're making frequent updates to multiple views on a very complex screen.

It's a very bad idea, however, to keep your views hanging around once your activity's onDestroy method has been invoked by the system. Making changes to a view that was once part of an expired activity will have dire consequences (force close dialogs, grumpy users, bad market reviews).

XML VS. JAVA LAYOUTS

On the whole, laying out your view in Java is nearly as simple as writing it out in XML. So, why would you put any layouts in XML?

The short answer is that Android has systems in place to load different XML layouts for you depending on the deployment device screen size and configuration. Do all this work in Java and you won't be able to take advantage of this massive time saver. Also, it takes a programmer to modify Java code, but most designers can beat the XML layouts into displayable shape. Although you might be the only one working on your current project, this will not be true for all your projects.

The longer answer to the question of XML versus Java layouts will become clear as you read the "Resource Management" section.

HANDLING A FEW COMMON TASKS

Some tasks are more common than others. Let's take a look at how you can handle some of the ones that you'll do a few dozen times before you finish your first application.

CHANGING THE VISIBILITY OF A VIEW

Most of the time, if you want to define your UI in XML you'll need to add views that will be visible only some of the time.

> **TIP:** If you find yourself doing this a lot, be sure to check out the `ViewStub` class.

Depending on how dynamic your application is, views come and go fairly regularly. Showing and hiding views is as simple as using the ever trusty `findViewById` and then calling `setVisibility` on the returned object:

```
Button button = (Button)findViewById(R.id.sample_button);

//Cycle through the View Visibility settings

if(button != null){

    //Gone (no impact on layouts)
    button.setVisibility(View.GONE);

    //Invisible (holds its space in a layout but is not drawn)
    button.setVsibility(View.INVISIBLE);

    //Visible (duh)
    button.setVisibility(View.VISIBLE);
}
```

This code has three visibility settings. GONE and VISIBLE are the most obvious. You'll find yourself using INVISIBLE less often, however it's great for keeping all the other views inside your layouts from moving around when you want to hide something.

SETTING AN ONCLICKLISTENER

Setting up a listener to tell you that one of your views has been clicked is one of the most common tasks you'll do when working on an Android application. A *click* can mean the user moved focus to your view using the navigation pad or trackball and then clicked the select key. A click can also mean pressing on the trackball, if there's one of those, or on the key in the center of the four- or eight-way directional pad.

Your click listener will also be called if, in touch mode, the user taps their finger down on your view and then lifts up with their finger still within the bounds of the view. This is an important distinction, as your click listener will not be invoked when their finger actually clicks down on the view but rather when the user lifts their finger up. This gives the user the chance to put a finger down in the wrong place and then correct the position before lifting it.

You can track view clicks in several ways. You can declare that your activity itself implements the view's OnClickListener interface, add a public void onClick (View v) method, and pass a pointer to your activity to the view you wish to track. Here's what that looks like in code for theoretical buttons with IDs button_one and button_two declared in an imaginary main.xml layout file:

```java
public class UiDemoActivity extends Activity implements
→   OnClickListener {

    @Override
    public void onClick(View selectedView) {
    if(selectedView.getId() == R.id.button_one){
        //Take Button One actions
    }
    if(selectedView.getId() == R.id.button_one){
        //Take Button Two actions
    }
}

    @Override
public void onCreate(Bundle savedInstanceState) {
    super.onCreate(savedInstanceState);
    setContentView(R.layout.main);
```

```
Button button = (Button)findViewById(R.id.button_one);
if(button != null)
    button.setOnClickListener(this);
Button button_two = (Button)findViewById(R.id.button_two);
if(button_two!= null)
    button_two.setOnClickListener(this);
}
```

There are two methods at work here. In the onCreate method that is called when the activity is being initialized, you'll see me pulling button_one and button_two out of the layout with findViewById. If the system correctly returned an instance, I register my activity (passing in a pointer to the activity with "this") as the click listener for each view.

Registering a click listener with a view does two things. First, it tells the system to call the appropriate onClick method. Second, it tells the system that this view accepts both focus (highlightable by the navigation buttons) and touch events. You can switch these states on or off by yourself with code, but setting a click listener ensures that click events can actually be *heard* by the view.

There's a second way to set up the same dynamic. This method sets up a new OnClickListener object for each view. This can help keep code separate if your screen has a lot of clickable items on it. Here's what this pattern looks like, and it achieves the same results as the previous code.

```
public class UiDemoActivity extends Activity{
    private View.OnClickListener mClickListenerOne =
new View.OnClickListener() {
        @Override
        public void onClick(View v) {
            //Do button one stuff here
        }
    };
    private View.OnClickListener mClickListenerTwo =
```

```
new View.OnClickListener() {
        @Override
        public void onClick(View v) {
            //Do button two stuff here
        }
    };
    @Override
    public void onCreate(Bundle savedInstanceState) {
        super.onCreate(savedInstanceState);
        setContentView(R.layout.main);
        Button button = (Button)findViewById(R.id.button_one);
        if(button != null)
            button.setOnClickListener(mClickListenerOne);
        Button button_two = (Button)findViewById(R.id.button_two);
        if(button_two!= null)
            button_two.setOnClickListener(mClickListenerTwo);
    }
}
```

This time, instead of declaring my activity as an implementer of the OnClick
Listener, I'm creating two separate inner objects to handle the click event from
each individual button. I'll put the code required for button_one in the first object
and the code for button_two in the second. I do this frequently in my own applications when I have several buttons on the screen. It keeps me from having one
heaping pile of if statements (or one switch statement) that figure out which view
was clicked and then take the appropriate action.

Depending on your needs, you can mix and match two techniques. There isn't
a huge advantage either way, but it's good to know each so you can keep your code
in good order.

In this example, I've added a click listener to two buttons. A click listener can be attached to any view that you want users to interact with. This can be anything from entire view groups to simple text views.

It's worth mentioning again that by setting a click listener, you're telling the system that the item can be selected (touched with a finger) and clicked (highlighted with the trackpad and then clicked with the center key or trackball). As a result, whatever default selection action is configured for the view will automatically run on a select event (either from the directional keypad or the touchscreen). Buttons, for example, change colors when a user selects them. Text views, depending on the device's default UI style, may also change the active color of the text. In the end, you can (and probably should) specify custom display behavior by declaring a state-full drawable. I'll show you how to do such things later in the book.

CREATING CUSTOM VIEWS

The concept of custom views can really be broken out into two sections: extending an existing view and creating an entirely new one. I've rarely, in my career as an Android developer, created a completely custom view, so we'll skip over it here. The Android SDK documentation has directions for the industrious among you who want to roll your very own from scratch. However, even if you plan to extend an Android view, you must create a new class that extends the existing view. Here's how you'd go about it.

DECLARING THE NEW CLASS
The first step in declaring a custom view is to create the class. Android allows you to subclass any of its existing UI objects simply by extending an existing class. The declaration looks like this:

```
public class CustomTextView extends TextView{

    public CustomTextView(Context context) {

        super(context);

    }

}
```

That's all it takes to create a custom text view. However, since there's about as much custom in this custom text view as there is beef in fast-food tacos, I'll add something simple to set it apart.

EXTENDING A VIEW

Although Android's layouts and views are powerful and versatile, there are times when they just won't do exactly what you want. Fortunately, their functionality is easy to extend. To demonstrate, I've written a custom text view that changes the color of every letter in the text to be displayed onscreen. While this isn't the most practical use case, it will show how simple it is to implement your own behavior.

CUSTOMIZING AN EXTENDED VIEW

You'd be amazed at how much code it takes to correctly render text to the screen. Android's TextView.java class is nearly 5000 lines of code. But thanks to the ability to extend a class, you can use all the complex layout code and customize only the part that appeals to you. In this example, I catch the text as it changes and add a new ForegroundColorSpan for each letter in the new string. First, I declare an array of colors.

```
public class CustomTextView extends TextView{

    int colorArray[] = new int[]{Color.WHITE,

        Color.RED,

        Color.YELLOW,

        Color.GREEN,

        Color.BLUE,

        Color.MAGENTA,

        Color.CYAN,

        Color.DKGRAY};
```

Now, each time the text changes, I add a new ForegroundColorSpan for each letter.

```
protected void onTextChanged(CharSequence text,
        int start, int before, int after )
{
    //Keep the view from getting into an infinite loop
    if(selfChange){
        selfChange = false;
        return;
    }
    selfChange=true;
}
```

I make sure I don't get stuck in an infinite loop (with the change in color triggering another onTextChanged call, which changes the color again, which changes the color…you get the idea). Next comes the code that changes the colors:

```
SpannableStringBuilder builder = new SpannableStringBuilder(text);
builder.clearSpans();
ForegroundColorSpan colorSpan;
int color;
for(int i=0; i < text.length(); i++){
    //pick the next color
    color = colorArray[i%colorArray.length];
    //Create the color span
    colorSpan = new ForegroundColorSpan(color);
    //Add the color span for this one char
    builder.setSpan(colorSpan,
                i, i,
                Spannable.SPAN_EXCLUSIVE_EXCLUSIVE);
}
setText(builder);
```

Again, not very complex, but then neither is extending an existing view class. Also, be warned that this code will clear any formatting that may have already been set on the text. (At this point, don't stress too much about how spans and SpannableStringBuilders work. In short, they're blocks of formatting that you can drop over strings. Check the Android SDK documentation for more info.) If you're looking for a coding challenge, try creating an array with every possible RGB hex color value and cycling through that array.

USING YOUR EXTENDED VIEW

Just as with any other Android view, you can create a new instance of it at runtime in your Java code or pre-declare it in your XML layout file. Here's how you can use it in your activity:

```java
public void onCreate(Bundle savedInstanceState) {

    super.onCreate(savedInstanceState);

    CustomTextView customView = new CustomTextView(this);

    customView.setText("Hello There!");

    setContentView(customView);

}
```

There's nothing you haven't seen before going on here. I'm creating a new instance of my view, setting the text for it, and then setting it as the main view for my activity. You could also put it inside a layout object with other views. It's also possible to add this custom view to an XML-described layout. But before you can start declaring your custom view in an XML file, you need to create the full suite of View constructors. Your custom view should look something like this:

```java
public class CustomTextView extends TextView{

    public CustomTextView(Context context,

                    AttributeSet attributeSet,

                    int defSytle)

    {

        super(context, attributeSet, defSytle);

    }
```

```java
    public CustomTextView(Context context,
                    AttributeSet attributeSet)
{
        super(context, attributeSet);
    }
    public CustomTextView(Context context){
        super(context);
    }
    //Rest of the class omitted for brevity
}
```

When Android parses your XML layout and creates your view, it needs to pass an attribute set to the constructor because this contains all the layout information, text, and whatever else you've added that starts with android. If you forget to add these, everything will compile, but it will show the Unexpected Force Close window of doom when you try to draw the screen.

Now that you have the correct constructors, it's possible to create and lay out your custom view within XML. In the code to follow, I've added a single instance of the rainbow animating custom text display.

```xml
<?xml version="1.0" encoding="utf-8"?>
<LinearLayout xmlns:android="http://schemas.android.com/apk/res/
→  android"
    android:orientation="vertical"
    android:layout_width="fill_parent"
    android:layout_height="fill_parent"
    >
    <com.haseman.ui.CustomTextView
        android:layout_width="wrap_content"
        android:layout_height="wrap_content"
        android:text="See how the colors change!"
    />
```

As you can see, adding a custom text view to your XML layouts only requires you to use the full Java package and class name. You can also see that because `CustomTextView` extends `TextView`, I can use any attribute (like `android:text`) that I would use with one of Android's `TextView`s.

Congrats, you've created a custom Android view to do your bidding in only a few lines of code, you've displayed it to the screen, and you even have the capability to include it within a more complex layout system. Google has done a fantastic job of allowing developers to extend the functionality of basic building blocks included in the Android SDK. If this extended custom view leaves you wanting more of a challenge, try making a simple text view that does exactly the same things as the extended view. You'll need to explore the `onMeasure` and `onDraw` methods of your own view. Go ahead, check it out, I'll be here when you get back.

RESOURCE MANAGEMENT

Android has many tools to help you manage string literals, images, layouts, and more. Moving all this constant data into external files makes life as a programmer easier in a multitude of ways. In previous code examples, I've referenced the `R.java` file when specifying strings, drawable images, and layouts and mentioned that an explanation would be forthcoming. Now is the time to explain Android resource management in detail.

RESOURCE FOLDER OVERVIEW

Every Android project, by default, contains a `res` folder with several subfolders inside it. Each subfolder is responsible for a different aspect of your application's data.

The drawable folders (`drawable-hdpi`, `drawable-mdpi`, and `drawable-ldpi`) hold images and XML files describing drawable objects. You'll learn much more about what you can do with drawable objects in later chapters.

The `values` folder holds all your textual content, from string literals to menu list value arrays to color constants.

Lastly, the layout folders contain XML files to describe how you want your screens to look.

At compile time, the Android tools take all the folders in your `res` directory and place a corresponding ID into an `R.java` file. This file is automatically re-created and placed in the project's gen folder. Consequently, you should never directly change this `R.java` file, because any changes are removed the next time you compile. The IDs in `R.java` can be passed to everything from XML parsers to text and image views. When you call `setText` on a `TextView` and pass in `R.string.hello`, the view then knows to look for that ID in the string file and display what it finds there. When you set the main view of an activity by calling `setContentView` and passing in `R.layout` `.main`, the system knows it needs to inflate and create the views found in `res/layout/ main.xml` and add them to the active views on the screen for the current activity.

Here's what the R.java file looks like for a newly created project:

```java
/* AUTO-GENERATED FILE. DO NOT MODIFY.
 *
 * This class was automatically generated by the
 * aapt tool from the resource data it found. It
 * should not be modified by hand.
 */
package com.haseman.peachpit;
public final class R {
    public static final class attr {
    }
    public static final class drawable {
        public static final int icon=0x7f020000;
    }
    public static final class layout {
        public static final int main=0x7f030000;
    }
    public static final class string {
        public static final int app_name=0x7f040001;
        public static final int hello=0x7f040000;
    }
}
```

When Android compiles your XML files, it renders them to a packed binary format. The upside of this format is that it loads much faster, so your screens can snap into focus more quickly. The downside is that you cannot modify any of these files once they've been compiled. So you can't manipulate your layout and string *files* at runtime. You can, however, modify what is rendered to the screen by loading and changing strings in the Java representation of the views.

Additionally, if you want to reference various resources from other XML files, you'll use the `@folder/object_id` structure. While you may not have been aware of it, you've seen this kind of declaration in action already. Think back to the initial Hello World layout that the Android tools provide for you. In it, you saw a text view with the following line: `android:text="@string/hello"`. This was Android's resource system at work. Instead of specifying `R.string.hello`, you'll use the XML's `@string/hello` for XML.

Each type of folder (drawable, layout, `values`, and several more) has special naming conventions and tricks you can use to battle the time-consuming problems of device diversity, language localization, and differing screen resolutions and densities. Let's look at what you can do with each type of file.

VALUES FOLDER

The prospect of putting all the constant values for your user interface (strings, colors, or int/string arrays) in a separate file might sound annoying at first (especially when you consider that all text manipulators will take a resource ID or a `CharSequence`). However, it can cut down many days of work when translating your application to different languages.

Having all your strings in an external XML file also means that your nontechnical colleagues (product managers, designers, or micromanaging bosses) can manipulate the display text in the screens, menus, and pop-up dialogs without bothering you. This assumes, of course, that you teach them how to compile and run the project; feel free to share the first chapter of this book with them.

The `values` folder can contain:

Strings. All string literals should go into your `strings.xml` file.

Arrays. There is a file for the XML-defined arrays, but string arrays can still go in the `strings.xml` file if you don't feel like using a separate file.

Colors. `colors.xml` can contain any number of declared color constants for use in everything from text fonts to layout backgrounds. Unless you're planning on doing a lot of custom UI drawing, this file will probably not be very large.

Dimensions. `dimens.xml` can contain any number of possible size values used elsewhere in your layouts. This file is particularly handy if you wish to make a view taller or shorter based on the display size of the device your application is being displayed on. This might seem like a simple thing to do, but it can be very powerful when combined with the layout folders.

Styles. `styles.xml`...yeah...more about this later.

You can create new `values` folders for each language by using the two-letter ISO639-2 suffix for a particular language as a suffix to `values`. You can, for example, create a `values-es` folder containing a Spanish version of the `strings.xml` file. When a user sets his or her phone to Spanish, Android will check automatically for an `R.string.hello` value defined in the `strings.xml` file within the new `values-es` folder. If it finds one, it will display the `values-es` version rather than the default. If it doesn't find a Spanish translation, it will default to the value you defined in `values/strings.xml`.

In this way, Android provides you with an easy way to localize all the strings in your application. It does, however, require you to be vigilant about placing your string literals in the `strings.xml` file rather than just calling `setText("Text like this");` or using `android:text="Text like this"` in your XML.

LAYOUT FOLDERS

I'm going to give you three guesses as to what exactly goes into the layout folders. Typically, it's where you place either layout XML files for use in `setContentView` calls, or sub-layouts that can be included via `ViewStubs` or inherited views (two tools that allow you to reuse views in different layouts). Android builds a helpful mechanic into the layout folders. You can have many folders, with different suffixes, that describe how you want the application to appear under various screen configurations.

The simplest example is a `layout` folder and a `layout-land` folder. If you place a `firstscreen.xml` file in both folders, Android will use the one that most closely resembles the current screen mode. If you keep the `android:id` settings consistent, you will be able to specify two completely different-looking screens within your XML markups and interact with any of them via your Java code. This technique is complicated, so let's look at an example.

Let's say you create portrait and landscape layouts for the first screen of your application. Both files are called `firstscreen.xml`, and the portrait version goes in the `layout` folder while the landscape version goes in the `layout-land` folder. You could also put the portrait version in a folder called `layout-port`. In both versions of `firstscreen.xml`, you provide all the appropriate IDs for the text views, buttons, and images.

If your screen had an OK button, you'd provide the portrait and landscape versions of these buttons the same ID: `R.id.ok_button`. Remember that you gain access to views by calling `findViewById()` and passing in the ID you specified on the `android:id="@+id/id_goes_here"` line. In this case, if you wanted to set a click listener, you'd fetch the OK button by calling `findViewById(R.id.ok_button);` and Android would return the button from your portrait screen if you're in portrait mode and the landscape version of the button if you're in landscape mode. Your code knows what it must do when that button is pressed, but it doesn't know about the dimensions or location of the button. Welcome to the happy land of the Model-View-Controller (MVC).

MVC is your number one friend when handling the diversity in device screen sizes. You can lay out your views in any possible configuration and, as long as the IDs match, you'll need to write only a single `Activity` class to handle all possible screen permutations. You can have specific folders, each with its own set of layout files for different screen sizes (layout-small to layout-xlarge) and densities (layout-ldpi to layout-hdpi), and you can mix and match. For example, layout-large-land would specify layouts for large screens (VGA and WVGA) that are in landscape mode. For the exact order in which Android defaults through the folders, be sure to check the Android SDK documentation.

I'm only scratching the surface of the possibilities that these layout folders put at your disposal. You'll learn more about this topic in coming chapters on dealing with display and hardware diversity.

DRAWABLE FOLDERS

For Android, a *drawable* is simply something that can be drawn to the screen. Android abstracts away the differences between colors, shapes, and images and allows you to deal with a superclass that can represent any number of them: Drawable.

You keep the definitions for these objects in the drawable folders.

You should consider using a drawable for two main types of objects:

- Image resources (mostly PNG files)

- XML files describing things you want drawn: shapes, gradients, or colors

The drawable set of folders works similarly to the layout folders. You can specify any mix of screen densities, layouts, or resolutions, provided you specify them in the right order.

MANY RESOURCES, ONE APK

Just because you can have a whole different set of images for each screen size or density doesn't mean you actually should. Keep a close eye on the size of your final compiled APK file. If the file grows over a certain size, users will complain. To combat this bloat, use 9-patches, which are easily scaled images, and use hand-rendered shapes over large PNG graphics where possible. While the new marketplace does allow for multiple APKs, it's a level of complexity you should avoid.

Referencing a drawable is accomplished in the same way that you reference values and layouts. For XML files, use the @drawable/resource_name. For example, in an ImageView (android:src="@drawable/bridge"), omit the suffix if you're referring to XML files or images. Also, keep in mind that Android will always try to use the drawable folder that is closest to your current configuration. If it can't find a good match, it'll cascade back to what it can find in the default drawable folder.

TIP: Be sure to check the Android SDK documentation for more info on ordering your suffixes correctly.

LAYOUT MANAGEMENT

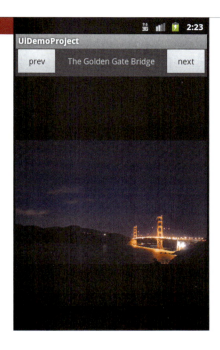

FIGURE 3.1 A taste of what's to come.

Layouts, from the simple to the complex, describe how to arrange a complex series of views. This section covers the basics of Android's arsenal of layout classes starting with the ViewGroup, moving through LinearLayouts, and ending with the king of the Android screen arrangers, the RelativeLayout.

THE VIEWGROUP

Each layout in Android extends what's known as the ViewGroup. This is the class of views that by definition can contain other views as children.

To demonstrate how each of the major layouts function, I'll be laying out an example picture-viewer screen. While Android provides its own snazzy photo viewer, complete with a thumbnail carousel, mine will be simple and an excellent vehicle for showing you how the various layouts work.

Figure 3.1 shows the screen that we'll be rendering using the AbsoluteLayout, the LinearLayout, and the RelativeLayout.

The example picture viewer has two sections: the button bar with title and the image itself. The button bar contains Next and Prev buttons and a text view displaying the name of the image.

Before getting too deep into the layout, there are a few terms to watch for in the XML:

> **dip** or **dp.** This is how Android helps you scale your screen layout to devices with different pixel densities. For example, on the Nexus S screen, 1dp = 1.5 pixels. It can be annoying to constantly convert the locations onscreen to dips, but this small investment in time will pay huge dividends when you're running on a multitude of Android screens. Example: `android:padding="20dp"`.
>
> **px.** Use this suffix to define an absolute pixel value for the specified dimension. In most cases, you should avoid declaring the absolute pixel value and use dp. Example: `android:paddingLeft="15px"`.
>
> **match_parent** and **wrap_content.** Before you can draw an Android view to the screen, it must have a defined `width` and `height`. You can define either of these two values as a constant value (20dp), or you can use one of the two special height and width values, `fill_parent` or `wrap_content`. Each value does exactly what you'd expect. `fill_parent` will make the view attempt to match the dimension of its parent. `wrap_content` will first request the measured size of the view and then attempt to set that dimension as the layout width for the view itself.

With a few simple definitions out of the way, I can start in on the various layout classes. I'll start with one that you'll find appealing but that you should never use in practice.

THE ABSOLUTELAYOUT

The most important thing you should know about `AbsoluteLayouts` is that you should never use them. They are the quintessential beginner's trap. They appear to be a good idea at first (as they quickly give you exact pixel design), but they can be frustrating, require excess time laying out new screens, and cause frequent face-desk interaction. Consult your local Android expert if you experience any of these side effects while trying to use an AbsoluteLayout. They'll likely try to talk you out of this lunacy.

The AbsoluteLayout, as you might have guessed, allows you to specify exactly where on the screen you want a particular view to go. Each child of an AbsoluteLayout should have android:layout_x and android:layout_y values along with the required width and height settings.

You are probably thinking, "That sounds like a great way to make layouts look exactly the way I want them to. Why bother learning anything else when I can take my screen designs and convert them directly into pixel x/y locations?"

I thought the same thing...at first.

Here's what the AbsoluteLayout layout XML looks like:

```xml
<?xml version="1.0" encoding="utf-8"?>
<AbsoluteLayout
    xmlns:android="http://schemas.android.com/apk/res/android"
    android:layout_width="match_parent"
    android:layout_height="match_parent">
    <Button
        android:id="@+id/prev"
        android:layout_width="wrap_content"
        android:layout_height="wrap_content"
        android:layout_x="0dp"
        android:layout_y="0dp"
        android:text="@string/prev_string"
        android:lines="1"
        android:padding="12dp"
        />
    <TextView
        android:id="@+id/url_view"
        android:layout_width="wrap_content"
```

```
            android:layout_height="wrap_content"
            android:layout_x="110dp"
            android:layout_y="0dp"
            android:gravity="center_horizontal"
            android:text="The Golden Gate"
            />
    <Button
            android:id="@+id/next"
            android:layout_width="wrap_content"
            android:layout_height="wrap_content"
            android:text="@string/next_string"
            android:layout_x="271dp"
            android:layout_y="0dp"
            android:lines="1"
            android:padding="12dp"
            />
    <ImageView
            android:layout_width="wrap_content"
            android:layout_height="wrap_content"
            android:layout_x="0dp"
            android:layout_y="20dp"
            android:gravity="center"
            android:id="@+id/main_image"
            android:src="@drawable/bridge"
            />
</AbsoluteLayout>
```

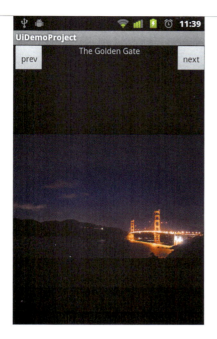

FIGURE 3.2 AbsoluteLayout (left) seems like a good idea at first…

FIGURE 3.3 This isn't good at all (right).

Nothing in this layout code should look shocking. Each button, text view, and image view has x and y coordinates. This simple code arranges the views to look very similar (**Figure 3.2**) to the original.

All right, Figure 3.2 looks similar to Figure 3.1, but hang on, this is only one of the 20-something ways that you can consume a single layout. Let's look at what happens to this layout when switching to landscape (**Figure 3.3**).

Yikes, that looks…bad! This is no way for a screen to look on any layout. Sure, you could do an alternative layout for every portrait and landscape screen out there, but that could add weeks to your schedule, and, worse, every time you need a new screen aspect you'll have to start from scratch.

While the AbsoluteLayout can give you a pixel-perfect design, it can achieve that look for only a single screen configuration. Given that Android has many dozens of screen sizes and types spread across a huge number of physical devices, layouts like these will make your life miserable once you move beyond your initial test device.

The only way to make life harder for yourself is to use an AbsoluteLayout with its children views defined in exact pixels (px) x and y values. Not only will a screen laid out in this way break when you switch to landscape, but it'll break when you switch from, say, the Nexus S to the HTC Hero, because they each have a different number of pixels on the screen.

I've included the AbsoluteLayout in this chapter because if I didn't, you might find it on your own and wonder at what a gem you'd found. This is a cautionary tale. The other layouts can be frustrating and time consuming up front, but trust me, they'll pay off in the end.

Bottom line: Don't use AbsoluteLayouts except for extremely simple cases. I could see it used to lay out a small, sophisticated button that could then be dropped into one of the more dynamic layout classes…but please, for your own sanity, don't use this layout object unless you absolutely cannot avoid it.

THE LINEARLAYOUT

A LinearLayout is the exact opposite of the AbsoluteLayout. Within it, you'll define a series of views, and the system will size and place them dynamically on the screen in the order you've specified. This layout is, and I cannot emphasize this enough, not very good for putting views exactly where you want them. I'm saving the layout class that is best at this for last.

Here's how the original picture viewer looks when designed to work with a LinearLayout:

```
<LinearLayout
    xmlns:android="http://schemas.android.com/apk/res/android"
    android:layout_width="match_parent"
    android:layout_height="match_parent"
    android:orientation="vertical"
    >
    <LinearLayout
        android:layout_width="match_parent"
        android:layout_height="wrap_content"
        android:orientation="horizontal"
        android:background="#333333"
        android:id="@+id/button_bar"
        >
```

```
    <Button
        android:id="@+id/prev"
        android:layout_width="wrap_content"
        android:layout_height="wrap_content"
        android:paddingLeft="5dip"
        android:paddingRight="5dip"
        android:text="@string/prev_string"
        android:lines="1"
        android:layout_weight="1"
        />
    <TextView
        android:id="@+id/url_view"
        android:layout_width="wrap_content"
        android:layout_height="wrap_content"
        android:gravity="center_horizontal"
        android:layout_weight="1"
        android:text="The Golden Gate Bridge"
        />
    <Button
        android:id="@+id/next"
        android:layout_width="wrap_content"
        android:layout_height="wrap_content"
        android:paddingLeft="5dip"
        android:paddingRight="5dip"
        android:text="@string/next_string"
        android:lines="1"
        android:layout_weight="1"/>
</LinearLayout>
<ImageView
```

```
        android:layout_width="wrap_content"

        android:layout_height="wrap_content"

        android:gravity="center_horizontal"

        android:id="@+id/main_image"

        android:src="@drawable/bridge"

        />

</LinearLayout>
```

Notice that there are two LinearLayouts at work in this example. The top-level layout contains the second LinearLayout object and the image to be displayed. The second LinearLayout contains the two buttons and the text of the title. Two layouts are required, in this case, because any one LinearLayout may have only one orientation.

DON'T GET IN TOO DEEP

LinearLayouts can only lay out their children in one of two orientations: horizontal or vertical. This can, if you're not careful, lead to screens with heaping piles of nested layout objects. Go too deep into a set of nested layouts and your screen will render at the speed of a herd of turtles. Android engineers suggest keeping the depth of your layout to less than ten. This is to say, don't create a view hierarchy with more than ten nested layouts of any kind. In practice, do everything you can to use as few layouts as possible, because you'll start to see slowdowns on older, slower phones when your layout depths are greater than seven or eight. If you find you've gotten in over your head with a stack of LinearLayouts, consider refactoring with a single RelativeLayout instead.

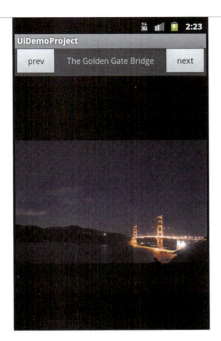

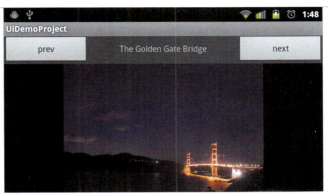

FIGURE 3.4 The LinearLayout-based screen (left).

FIGURE 3.5 The same layout but in landscape (right).

Figure 3.4 shows what this example XML produces in portrait mode.

This is where Android's dynamic layouts really start to shine; take a look at what the exact same layout code looks like when the user shifts into landscape mode (**Figure 3.5**).

Not perfect, but a vast improvement over the AbsoluteLayout's version of the landscape screen.

USING LINEARLAYOUTS

When using the LinearLayout, the order in which you define your views is the order in which they're placed on the screen. First, take a look at that second LinearLayout:

```
<LinearLayout
    android:layout_width="match_parent"
    android:layout_height="wrap_content"
    android:orientation="horizontal"
    android:background="#333333"
    android:id="@+id/button_bar"
>
```

ONE VIEW MUST BE IN CHARGE OF SIZE

One view, or layout, must define a height and width value. You cannot tell Android that you'd like a layout to wrap its content while, at the same time, telling a view that it should match its parent. This will cause a compile error because Android has no idea how big to make either the parent view or the child layout. Something must define an actual height, even if it's an image or a line of text.

By setting the orientation to horizontal, Android knows to place the children in order from left to right across the top of the screen. The outer layout is a vertical one, allowing placement of the button bar above the image.

By setting the width to match_parent, I'm making sure the layout itself stretches all the way across the parent layout (in this case the entire screen). The height is set to wrap_content, so it will be exactly as tall as the final measured height of its children.

The LinearLayout distributes its children in the order they're defined. It then measures all the child views to see how much space they'd like to take up. It will then divvy up the available space in proportion to the ideal size of its children. If there is too little space to accommodate all the child views, it'll give each child a part of their required space in proportion to their measured size. If there's more than enough space for all the child views, it'll pass out the extra space based on how large the child's onMeasure call tells the layout it wants to be. You can modify this proportional distribution through the layout_weight attribute in each child.

Layout really happens more in the definition of the children than the declaration of the layout itself. So, for a bit of context, let's take a look at the individual members of the button bar layout.

Here is the first of the child views in the definition for the Prev button:

FIGURE 3.6 Overly large buttons thanks to the LinearLayout.

```
<Button
    android:id="@+id/prev"
    android:layout_width="wrap_content"
    android:layout_height="wrap_content"
    android:paddingLeft="5dip"
    android:paddingRight="5dip"
    android:text="@string/prev_string"
    android:lines="1"
    android:layout_weight="1"
    />
```

The layout_weight value, which can be any decimal number from 0 to 1, tells the system how much space to give to the child view when the layout has either too much or too little space.

Take a look at the landscape version of the button bar again (**Figure 3.6**).

LINEAR LAYOUTS ARE **NOT** FOR PIXEL **PERFECTIONISTS**

I've said it once and I'll now say it a second time: LinearLayouts are not great for laying out pixel-perfect screens. As views get proportionally larger and smaller, it becomes difficult to get them to rest exactly where you want them to. Use the LinearLayout when you have a known quantity of objects that must get on the screen and you're not overly picky about exactly where they end up. In small, space-constrained cases, as with small button bars or single list menu entries, AbsoluteLayouts *can* prove to be much easier to use to get exactly the screen layout you're looking for. This might be the only case I can think of where an AbsoluteLayout *might* make sense.

FIGURE 3.7 Oops, too small!

This may be very close to the way the screen looks in portrait mode, but not close enough. As the top bar grows, the LinearLayout hands out extra pixel space in proportion to the measured size of the child view. In this case, because all three elements (two buttons and the text title) are weighted the same (1), the layout divides the extra space evenly among them. You can re-weight the buttons such that they grow in different ratios to the text title. Since you want the buttons to grow at a slower rate than the text, you could try setting their weights to 0. Here are what the new values look like (with everything else omitted):

```
<LinearLayout

>

    <Button

        android:layout_weight="0"

        />

    <TextView

        android:layout_weight="1"

        />

    <Button

        android:layout_weight="0"

/>

</LinearLayout>
```

Figure 3.7 shows what this change does to the button bar.

Well, technically that's correct, but it looks awful. You have two options. You can declare exactly how much extra space you'd like each of the two buttons to have through the android:padding declaration, or you can give them a little bit more weight. You can fiddle with the first option on your own, but let's take a look at the padding option together.

While you don't want the buttons to get too large, you still need to give them a bit more space than exactly what fits around the text. Let's try .25 for a `weight`. I've pulled out all non-`layout_weight` lines for brevity:

```
<LinearLayout>

    <Button

        android:layout_weight=".25"

        />

    <TextView

        android:layout_weight="1"

        />

    <Button

        android:layout_weight=".25"

        />

/>

</LinearLayout>
```

FIGURE 3.8 That's much better!

FIGURE 3.9 Check back in on portrait mode.

Figure 3.8 shows how that looks in landscape mode.

The result is much more reasonable. But to be sure, check what the bar looks like in portrait mode. **Figure 3.9** shows the result.

Perhaps the Next and Prev buttons could be a little bit larger in portrait mode, but this result is more than acceptable. They're not huge, they don't look crowded, and they should be big enough even for large fingers to hit.

In the end, nothing beats the `LinearLayout`s for easily handling different dynamic screen sizes. Throw as much into one as you please, and it'll try to accommodate everything. There are, however, two major issues to watch out for. First, because they can orient themselves in only one direction, you may end up needing a lot of them to handle a complex layout, which can slow drawing performance significantly. Second, getting a complex screen to render exactly as your designer wants it to can be an intensive process. For more complex or busy screens and objects, you're much better off using a `RelativeLayout`.

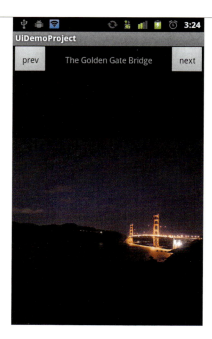

FIGURE 3.10 Designing the same screen, except with the RelativeLayout.

THE RELATIVELAYOUT

The RelativeLayout is the mack daddy of the Android screen layout system. It allows you to position all your child views in relation to either the parent (the layout itself) or any other child view within the layout. Let's take a look at one in action. Here's the now familiar image and button arrangement in the photo viewer, but with a RelativeLayout (**Figure 3.10**).

There are a few slight measurement differences between this image and the one produced with the LinearLayout. This one is also missing the gray background behind the buttons, which I'll show you how to add shortly.

Take a look at the XML layout that produced the image in Figure 3.10.

```xml
<?xml version="1.0" encoding="utf-8"?>

<RelativeLayout

    xmlns:android="http://schemas.android.com/apk/res/android"

    android:layout_width="match_parent"

    android:layout_height="match_parent">
```

```
<Button
    android:id="@+id/prev"
    android:layout_width="wrap_content"
    android:layout_height="wrap_content"
    android:padding="15dip"
    android:text="@string/prev_string"
    android:layout_alignParentLeft="true"
    android:layout_alignParentTop="true"
    />
<Button
    android:id="@+id/next"
    android:layout_width="wrap_content"
    android:layout_height="wrap_content"
    android:padding="15dip"
    android:text="@string/next_string"
    android:layout_alignParentRight="true"
    android:layout_alignParentTop="true"
    />
<TextView
    android:id="@+id/text_view"
    android:layout_width="wrap_content"
    android:layout_height="wrap_content"
    android:gravity="center"
    android:layout_toRightOf="@id/prev"
    android:layout_toLeftOf="@id/next"
    android:layout_alignParentTop="true"
    android:layout_centerHorizontal="true"
    android:layout_alignBottom="@id/prev"
```

```
        android:text="The Golden Gate Bridge"
        />
    <ImageView
        android:layout_width="wrap_content"
        android:layout_height="wrap_content"
        android:layout_alignParentLeft="true"
        android:layout_alignParentRight="true"
        android:layout_below="@id/text_view"
        android:gravity="center"
        android:id="@+id/main_image"
        android:src="@drawable/bridge"
        />
</RelativeLayout>
```

In this layout code, you see the same view components that made up the Linear Layout except, with the relative version, there's no need for a second, nested layout. The mechanics to each member of a RelativeLayout can be more complex than its linear cousin, so I'll endeavor to break down all four pieces of this screen one at a time.

The <RelativeLayout> declaration contains only enough information to tell the layout to fill the entire screen. All information on how to lay out the screen is found in the child elements. Here's the first one:

```
<Button
    android:id="@+id/prev"
    android:layout_width="wrap_content"
    android:layout_height="wrap_content"
    android:padding="15dip"
    android:text="@string/prev_string"
    android:layout_alignParentLeft="true"
    android:layout_alignParentTop="true"
    />
```

The first view, which declares the Prev button, initially declares its ID in the android:id line. The Prev button needs an ID so you can assign a click listener to it in the activity code. The layout height and width declarations simply tell the view to make it large enough to accommodate all the content (in this case, the "prev" text and a little padding).

The padding declaration tells the system to push the boundaries for the button out from the smallest required space for the text. In this case, android:padding="15dip" tells the system to measure the required space for the "prev" text and then 15 more device-independent pixels to the outer boundary of the view. As a general rule, it's always good to pad your buttons between 10 and 20 dip (depending on screen and text size). This gives them a little more space to be recognized as buttons, and it also gives people with large fingers a chance of actually hitting the view.

Now come the parts that tell the system where inside the layout object to place the button. The attribute android:layout_alignParentLeft="true" tells Android to align the left edge of the view with the left edge of the parent's bounding rectangle. In this case, it's the left edge of the screen. The android:layout_alignParentTop="true" attribute does the same thing except with respect to the top of the layout object (in this case, the top of the application's available space).

If you don't specify any layout parameters, views will default to the upper-left corner of the layout object. This code example declares these views for explanation purposes.

Now that the Prev button is in place, you're ready to move on. Here's the relevant XML for the Next button:

```
<Button
    android:id="@+id/next"
    android:layout_width="wrap_content"
    android:layout_height="wrap_content"
    android:padding="15dip"
    android:text="@string/next_string"
    android:layout_alignParentRight="true"
    android:layout_alignParentTop="true"
    />
```

The Next button is nearly identical to the Prev button except for the ID (required to set up a click listener in the activity), the text displaying on the button ("next"), and the android:layout_alignParentRight="true" attribute (to lock it to the right side of the layout object—and thus the right side of the screen—instead of the left). Here's the code for the title:

```
<TextView
    android:id="@+id/text_view"
    android:layout_width="wrap_content"
    android:layout_height="wrap_content"
    android:layout_toRightOf="@id/prev"
    android:layout_toLeftOf="@id/next"
    android:layout_alignParentTop="true"
    android:layout_centerHorizontal="true"
    android:layout_alignBottom="@id/prev"
    android:text="The Golden Gate Bridge"
    android:gravity="center"
    />
```

In this text view, things start to get a little more interesting. Again, the ID, height, and width are things you've seen before, but you need to change the title text as the images change. As the image changes, you'll need an ID so the activity can change the name of the picture displayed above it.

android:layout_toRightOf="@id/prev" tells the layout to align the left edge of the text view with the right edge of the Prev button. android:layout_toLeftOf= "@id/next" tells the right edge of the text view to align with the left-most edge of the Next button. The android:gravity="center" attribute tells the text to center itself within any extra available space. This will center it vertically (so it doesn't stick to the top of the screen) and horizontally (so it doesn't stick against the left-most button).

This technique of centering a view in the space between two objects is one I use frequently in my Android work, and it's a good way to eat up extra space caused by small and large fluctuations in screen size. That is to say, the text in the center of the buttons will float, centered, within any available screen space you might get when using a larger screen than the one you're designing.

ADDING THAT GRAY BACKGROUND

So, you might be asking, the LinearLayout example has a gray background; if the RelativeLayout is so amazing, why doesn't it have one as well? First, stop asking your book questions; you'll look a little odd in public. Second, I withheld the background because I wanted to show you how easy it is to add it. I've placed the XML required to add the background in the following code. Take a second to look it over:

```
<!-- This is the top level layout -->
<RelativeLayout
    xmlns:android="http://schemas.android.com/apk/res/android"
    android:layout_width="match_parent"
    android:layout_height="match_parent">
    <View
        android:layout_width="match_parent"
        android:layout_height="wrap_content"
        android:layout_alignParentLeft="true"
        android:layout_alignParentRight="true"
        android:layout_alignParentTop="true"
        android:layout_alignBottom="@id/next"
        android:background="#ff222222"
    />
    <!--Rest of the screen goes here -->
</RelativeLayout>
```

I want the gray box to be drawn behind the button bar, so I placed it as the first view in the layout. Android draws the view stack in the order they're declared. So, were I to incorrectly place the listed XML below the button and text declarations, you'd see only the gray bar covering over both the text and the buttons.

With that, you've successfully added a gray background and brought the Relative Layout version of this view into parity with the earlier LinearLayout demonstration. The RelativeLayout can handle more complex displays without requiring other nested layouts. It also can, if you're smart about it, handle changes in screen size, as shown by having the image's name float between the buttons no matter how far apart they get.

WRAPPING **UP**

Throughout this chapter, you've come to understand the fundamental building blocks that make up Android's UI. While I haven't yet had time to show you any of these particular classes in much depth, together we've laid the groundwork for more serious chapters to come. In this way I can dive deep into text views (yes, we will) without worrying that you'll not know how to arrange them next to an image or make them respond to click events.

This concludes the overview of displaying information to users. You should be comfortable building and changing basic user interfaces through Java and Android's XML layout system. If you didn't skip any sections, you'll also be able to extend existing built-in views to make Android do exactly your bidding. Next you'll take a break from drawing things on screens and look at how to acquire data for your pretty user interfaces.

4

ACQUIRING **DATA**

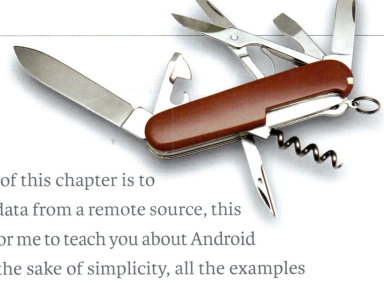

While the prime directive of this chapter is to teach you how to acquire data from a remote source, this is really just a sneaky way for me to teach you about Android and the main thread. For the sake of simplicity, all the examples in this chapter will deal with downloading and rendering image data. In the next chapter, on adapters and lists, I'll introduce you to parsing complex data and displaying it to users. Image data, as a general rule, is larger and more cumbersome, so you'll run into more interesting and demonstrative timing issues in dealing with it.

THE **MAIN THREAD**

The Android operation system has exactly one blessed thread authorized to change anything that will be seen by the user. This alleviates what could be a concurrency nightmare, such as view locations and data changing in one thread while a different one is trying to lay them out onscreen. If only one thread is allowed to touch the user interface, Android can guarantee that nothing vital is changed while it's measuring views and rendering them to the screen. This has, unfortunately, serious repercussions for how you'll need to acquire and process data. Let me start with a simple example.

YOU THERE, FETCH ME THAT DATA!

Were I to ask you, right now, to download an image and display it to the screen, you'd probably write code that looks a lot like this:

```
public void onCreate(Bundle extra){
try{

        URL url = new URL("http://wanderingoak.net/bridge.png");
        HttpURLConnection httpCon =
            (HttpURLConnection)url.openConnection();
        if(httpCon.getResponseCode() != 200)
        throw new Exception("Failed to connect");
        InputStream is = httpCon.getInputStream();
        Bitmap bitmap = BitmapFactory.decodeStream(is);
        ImageView iv = (ImageView)findViewById(R.id.main_image);
        if(iv!=null)
            iv.setImageBitmap(bitmap);
    }catch(Exception e){
    Log.e("ImageFetching","Didn't work!",e);
    }
}
```

FIGURE 4.1 What the user sees when you hold the main thread hostage.

This is exactly what I did when initially faced with the same problem. While this code will fetch and display the required bitmap, there is a very sinister issue lurking in the code—namely, the code itself is running on the main thread. Why is this a problem? Consider that there can be only one main thread and that the main thread is the only one that can interact with the screen in any capacity. This means that while the example code is waiting for the network to come back with image data, nothing whatsoever can be rendered to the screen. This image-fetching code will block any action from taking place anywhere on the device. If you hold the main thread hostage, buttons will not be processed, phone calls cannot be answered, and nothing can be drawn to the screen until you release it.

WATCHDOGS

Given that a simple programmer error (like the one in the example code) could effectively cripple any Android device, Google has gone to great lengths to make sure no single application can control the main thread for any length of time. Hogging too much of the main thread's time will result in this disastrous dialog screen (**Figure 4.1**) showing up over your application.

This dialog is unaffectionately referred to by developers as an ANR (App Not Responding) crash. Although operations will continue in the background, and the user can press the Wait button to return to whatever's going on within your application, this is catastrophic for most users, and you should avoid it at all costs.

WHAT NOT TO DO

What kind of things should you avoid on the main thread?

- Anything involving the network
- Any task requiring a read or write from or to the file system
- Heavy processing of any kind (such as image or movie modification)
- Any task blocking a thread while you wait for something to complete

Excluding this list, there isn't much left, so, as a general rule, if it doesn't involve setup or modification of the user interface, *don't* do it on the main thread.

WHEN AM I ON THE MAIN THREAD?

Anytime a method is called from the system (unless explicitly otherwise stated), you can be sure you're on the main thread. Again, as a general rule, if you're not in a thread created by you, it's safe to assume you're probably on the main one, so be careful.

GETTING OFF THE MAIN THREAD

You can see why holding the main thread hostage while grabbing a silly picture of the Golden Gate Bridge is a bad idea. But how, you might be wondering, do I get off the main thread? An inventive hacker might simply move all the offending code into a separate thread. This imaginary hacker might produce code looking something like this:

```
public void onCreate(Bundle extra){
new Thread(){
        public void run(){
            try{
                URL url = new URL("http://wanderingoak.net/bridge.
                → png");
                HttpURLConnection httpCon = (HttpURLConnection)
                → url.openConnection();
                if(httpCon.getResponseCode() != 200)
                    throw new
                    Exception("Failed to connect");
                InputStream is = httpCon.getInputStream();
                Bitmap bt = BitmapFactory.decodeStream(is);
                ImageView iv =
                (ImageView)findViewById(R.id.remote_image);
                iv.setImageBitmap(bt);
            }catch(Exception e){
                //handle failure here
            }
        }
    }.start();
}
```

"There," your enterprising hacker friend might say, "I've fixed your problem. The main thread can continue to run unimpeded by the silly PNG downloading code." There is, however, another problem with this new code. If you run the method on your own emulator, you'll see that it throws an exception and cannot display the image onscreen.

Why, you might now ask, is this new failure happening? Well, remember that the main thread is the only one allowed to make changes to the user interface? Calling setImageBitmap is very much in the realm of one of those changes and, thus, can be done only while on the main thread.

GETTING BACK TO MAIN LAND

Android provides, through the Activity class, a way to get back on the main thread as long as you have access to an activity. Let me fix the hacker's code to do this correctly. As I don't want to indent the code into the following page, I'll continue this from the line on which the bitmap is created (remember, we're still inside the Activity class, within the onCreate method, inside an inline thread declaration) (why do I hear the music from *Inception* playing in my head?).

For orientation purposes, I'll continue this from the line on which the bitmap was created in the previous code listing. If you're confused, check the sample code for this chapter.

```
final Bitmap bt = BitmapFactory.decodeStream(is);
ImageActivity.this.runOnUiThread(new Runnable() {
public void run() {
    ImageView iv = (ImageView)findViewById(R.id.remote_image);
        iv.setImageBitmap(bt);
        }
    });
//All the close brackets omitted to save space
```

Remember, we're already running in a thread, so accessing just `this` will refer to the thread itself. I, on the other hand, need to invoke a method on the activity. Calling `ImageActivity.this` provides a pointer to the outer `Activity` class in which we've spun up this hacky code and will thus allow us to call `runOnUiThread`. Further, because I want to access the recently created bitmap in a different thread, I'll need to make the bitmap declaration `final` or the compiler will get cranky with us.

When you call `runOnUiThread`, Android will schedule this work to be done as soon as the main thread is free from other tasks. Once back on the main thread, all the same "don't be a hog" rules again apply.

THERE MUST BE A BETTER WAY!

If you're looking at this jumbled, confusing, un-cancelable code and thinking to yourself, "Self. There must be a cleaner way to do this," you'd be right. There are many ways to handle long-running tasks; I'll show you what I think are the two most useful. One is the `AsyncTask`, a simple way to do an easy action within an activity. The other, `IntentService`, is more complicated but much better at handling repetitive work that can span multiple activities.

THE **ASYNCTASK**

At its core, the AsyncTask is an abstract class that you extend and that provides the basic framework for a time-consuming asynchronous task.

The best way to describe the AsyncTask is to call it a working thread sandwich. That is to say, it has three major methods for which you must provide implementation.

1. onPreExecute takes place on the main thread and is the first slice of bread. It sets up the task, prepares a loading dialog, and warns the user that something is about to happen.

2. doInBackground is the meat of this little task sandwich. This method is guaranteed by Android to run on a separate background thread. This is where the majority of your work takes place.

3. onPostExecute will be called once your work is finished (again, on the main thread), and the results produced by the background method will be passed to it. This is the other slice of bread.

That's the gist of the asynchronous task. There are more-complicated factors that I'll touch on in just a minute, but this is one of the fundamental building blocks of the Android platform (given that all hard work must be taken off the main thread).

Take a look at one in action, then we'll go over the specifics of it:

```
private class ImageDownloader
extends AsyncTask<String, Integer, Bitmap>{
protected void onPreExecute(){
    //Setup is done here
}
@Override
protected Bitmap doInBackground(String... params) {
    // TODO Auto-generated method stub
    try{
        URL url = new URL(params[0]);
```

```
            HttpURLConnection httpCon =
            (HttpURLConnection)url.openConnection();
            if(httpCon.getResponseCode() != 200)
                throw new Exception("Failed to connect");
            InputStream is = httpCon.getInputStream();
            return BitmapFactory.decodeStream(is);
        }catch(Exception e){
            Log.e("Image","Failed to load image",e);
        }
        return null;
    }
    protected void onProgressUpdate(Integer... params){
        //Update a progress bar here, or ignore it, it's up to you
    }
    protected void onPostExecute(Bitmap img){
        ImageView iv = (ImageView)findViewById(R.id.remote_image);
        if(iv!=null && img!=null){
            iv.setImageBitmap(img);
        }
    }
        protected void onCancelled(){
        }
    }
```

That, dear readers, is an asynchronous task that will download an image at the end of any URL and display it for your pleasure (provided you have an image view onscreen with the ID remote_image). Here is how you'd kick off such a task from the onCreate method of your activity.

```
public void onCreate(Bundle extras){

    super.onCreate(extras);

    setContentView(R.layout.image_layout);

    id = new ImageDownloader();

    id.execute("http://wanderingoak.net/bridge.png");

}
```

Once you call execute on the ImageDownloader, it will download the image, process it into a bitmap, and display it to the screen. That is, assuming your image_layout.xml file contains an ImageView with the ID remote_image.

HOW TO MAKE IT WORK FOR YOU

The AsyncTask requires that you specify three generic type arguments (if you're unsure about Java and generics, do a little Googling before you press on) as you declare your extension of the task.

- The type of parameter that will be passed into the class. In this example AsyncTask code, I'm passing one string that will be the URL, but I could pass several of them. The parameters will always be referenced as an array no matter how many of them you pass in. Notice that I reference the single URL string as params[0].

- The object passed between the doInBackground method (*off* the main thread) and the onProgressUpdate method (which will be called *on* the main thread). It doesn't matter in the example, because I'm not doing any progress updates in this demo, but it'd probably be an integer, which would be either the percentage of completion of the transaction or the number of bytes transferred.

- The object that will be returned by the doInBackground method to be handled by the onPostExecute call. In this little example, it's the bitmap we set out to download.

Here's the line in which all three objects are declared:

```
private class ImageDownloader extends
    AsyncTask<String, Integer, Bitmap>{
```

In this example, these are the classes that will be passed to your three major methods.

ONPREEXECUTE

```
protected void onPreExecute(){
}
```

onPreExecute is usually when you'll want to set up a loading dialog or a loading spinner in the corner of the screen (I'll discuss dialogs in depth later). Remember, onPreExecute is called on the main thread, so don't touch the file system or network at all in this method.

DOINBACKGROUND

```
protected Bitmap doInBackground(String... params) {
}
```

This is your chance to make as many network connections, file system accesses, or other lengthy operations as you like without holding up the phone. The class of object passed to this method will be determined by the first generic object in your AsyncTask's class declaration. Although I'm using only one parameter in the code sample, you can actually pass any number of parameters (as long as they derive from the saved class) and you'll have them at your fingertips when doInBackground is called. Once your long-running task has been completed, you'll need to return the result at the end of your function. This final value will be passed into another method called back on the main UI thread.

BEWARE LOADING DIALOGS

Remember that mobile applications are not like their web or desktop counterparts. Your users will typically be using their phones when they're away from a conventional computer. This means, usually, that they're already waiting for something: a bus, that cup of expensive coffee, their friend to come back from the bathroom, or a boring meeting to end. It's very important, therefore, to keep them from having to wait on anything within your application. Waiting for your mobile application to connect while you're already waiting for something else can be a frustrating experience. Do what you can to limit users' exposure to full-screen loading dialogs. They're unavoidable sometimes, but minimize them whenever possible.

SHOWING YOUR PROGRESS

There's another aspect of the AsyncTask that you should be aware of even though I haven't demonstrated it. From within doInBackground, you can send progress updates to the user interface. doInBackground isn't on the main thread, so if you'd like to update a progress bar or change the state of something on the screen, you'll have to get back on the main thread to make the change.

Within the AsyncTask, you can do this during the doInBackground method by calling publishProgress and passing in any number of objects deriving from the second class in the AsyncTask declaration (in the case of this example, an integer). Android will then, on the main thread, call your declared onProgressUpdate method and hand over any classes you passed to publishProgress. Here's what the method looks like in the AsyncTask example:

```
protected void onProgressUpdate(Integer... params){
    //Update a progress bar here, or ignore it, it's up to you
}
```

As always, be careful when doing UI updates, because if the activity isn't currently onscreen or has been destroyed, you could run into some trouble.

ONPOSTEXECUTE

The work has been finished or, in the example, the image has been downloaded. It's time to update the screen with what I've acquired. At the end of doInBackground, if successful, I return a loaded bitmap to the AsyncTask. Now Android will switch to the main thread and call onPostExecute, passing the class I returned at the end of doInBackground. Here's what the code for that method looks like:

```
protected void onPostExecute(Bitmap img){
    ImageView iv = (ImageView)findViewById(R.id.remote_image);
    if(iv!=null && img!=null){
        iv.setImageBitmap(img);
    }
}
```

I take the bitmap downloaded from the website, retrieve the image view into which it's going to be loaded, and set it as that view's bitmap to be rendered. There's an error case I haven't correctly handled here. Take a second to look back at the original code and see if you can spot it.

A FEW IMPORTANT CAVEATS

Typically, an AsyncTask is started from within an activity. However, you must remember that activities can have short life spans. Recall that, by default, Android destroys and re-creates any activity each time you rotate the screen. Android will also destroy your activity when the user backs out of it. You might reasonably ask, "If I start an AsyncTask from within an activity and then that activity is destroyed, what happens?" You guessed it: very bad things. Trying to draw to an activity that's already been removed from the screen can cause all manner of havoc (usually in the form of unhandled exceptions).

It's a good idea to keep track of any AsyncTasks you've started, and when the activity's onDestroy method is called, make sure to call cancel on any lingering AsyncTask.

There are a few cases in which the AsyncTask is perfect for the job:

- Downloading small amounts of data specific to one particular activity

- Loading files from an external storage drive (usually an SD card)

Make sure, basically, that the data you're moving with the AsyncTask pertains to only one activity, because your task generally shouldn't span more than one. You can pass it between activities if the screen has been rotated, but this can be tricky. There are a few cases when it's not a good idea to use an AsyncTask:

- Any acquired data that may pertain to more than one activity shouldn't be acquired through an AsyncTask. Both an image that might be shown on more than one screen and a list of messages in a Twitter application, for example, would have relevance outside a single activity.

- Data to be posted to a web service is also a bad idea to put on an AsyncTask for the following reason: Users will want to fire off a post (posting a photo, blog, tweet, or other data) and do something else, rather than waiting for a progress bar to clear. By using an AsyncTask, you're forcing them to wait around for the posting activity to finish.

- Last, be aware that there is some overhead for the system in setting up the AsyncTask. This is fine if you use a few of them, but it may start to slow down your main thread if you're firing off hundreds of them.

You might be curious as to exactly what you should use in these cases. I'm glad you are, because that's exactly what I'd like to show you next.

THE INTENTSERVICE

The IntentService is an excellent way to move large amounts of data around without relying on any specific activity or even application. The AsyncTask will always take over the main thread at least twice (with its pre- and post-execute methods), and it must be owned by an activity that is able to draw to the screen. The IntentService has no such restriction. To demonstrate, I'll show you how to download the same image, this time from the IntentService rather than the AsyncTask.

DECLARING A SERVICE

Services are, essentially, classes that run in the background with no access to the screen. In order for the system to find your service when required, you'll need to declare it in your manifest, like so:

```
<?xml version="1.0" encoding="utf-8"?>
<manifest xmlns:android="http://schemas.android.com/apk/res/android"
        package="com.haseman.Example"
        android:versionCode="1"
        android:versionName="1.0">
    <application
        android:name="MyApplication"
        android:icon="@drawable/icon"
        android:label="@string/app_name">
    <!—Rest of the application declarations go here -->
        <service android:name=".ImageIntentService"/>
    </application>
</manifest>
```

At a minimum, you'll need to have this simple declaration. It will then allow you to (as I showed you earlier with activities) explicitly launch your service. Here's the code to do exactly that:

```
Intent i = new Intent(this, ImageIntentService.class);
i.putExtra("url", getIntent().getExtras().getString("url"));
startService(i);
```

At this point, the system will construct a new instance of your service, call its onCreate method, and then start firing data at the IntentService's handleIntent method. The intent service is specifically constructed to handle large amounts of work and processing off the main thread. The service's onCreate method *will* be called on the main thread, but subsequent calls to handleIntent are guaranteed by Android to be on a background thread (and this is where you should put your long-running code in any case).

Right, enough gabbing. Let me introduce you to the ImageIntentService. The first thing you'll need to pay attention to is the constructor:

```
public class ImageIntentService extends IntentService{
    public ImageIntentService() {
        super("ImageIntentService");
    }
}
```

Notice that the constructor you must declare has no string as a parameter. The parent's constructor that you must call, however, must be passed a string. Eclipse will make it seem that you must declare a constructor with a string when, in reality, you must declare it without one. This simple mistake can cause you several hours of intense face-to-desk debugging.

Once your service exists, and before anything else runs, the system will call your onCreate method. onCreate is an excellent time to run any housekeeping chores you'll need for the rest of the service's tasks (more on this when I show you the image downloader).

At last, the service can get down to doing some heavy lifting. Once it has been constructed and has had its onCreate method called, it will then receive a call to handleIntent for each time any other activity has called startService.

FETCHING IMAGES

The main difference between fetching images and fetching smaller, manageable data is that larger data sets (such as images or larger data retrievals) should not be bundled into a final broadcast intent (another major difference to the AsyncTask). Also, keep in mind that the service has no direct access to any activity, so it cannot ever access the screen on its own. Instead of modifying the screen, the IntentService will send a broadcast intent alerting all listeners that the image download is complete. Further, since the service cannot pass the actual image data along with that intent, you'll need to save the image to the SD card and include the path to that file in the final completion broadcast.

THE SETUP

Before you can use the external storage to cache the data, you'll need to create a cache folder for your application. A good place to check is when the IntentService's onCreate method is called:

```java
public void onCreate(){
    super.onCreate();
    String tmpLocation =
        Environment.getExternalStorageDirectory().getPath()
        + CACHE_FOLDER;
    cacheDir = new File(tmpLocation);
    if(!cacheDir.exists()){
        cacheDir.mkdirs();
    }
}
```

Using Android's environment, you can determine the correct prefix for the external file system. Once you know the path to the eventual cache folder, you can then make sure the directory is in place. Yes, I know I told you to avoid file-system contact while on the main thread (and onCreate is called on the main thread), but checking and creating a directory is a small enough task that it should be all right. I'll leave this as an open question for you as you read through the rest of this chapter: Where might be a better place to put this code?

Relying on a file-system cache has an interesting twist with Android. On most phones, the internal storage space (used to install applications) is incredibly limited. You should not, under any circumstances, store large amounts of data anywhere on the local file system. Always save it to a location returned from getExternalStorageDirectory.

When you're saving files to the SD card, you must also be aware that nearly all pre-2.3 Android devices can have their SD cards removed (or mounted as a USB drive on the user's laptop). This means you'll need to gracefully handle the case where the SD card is missing. You'll also need to be able to forgo the file-system cache on the fly if you want your application to work correctly when the external drive is missing. There are a lot of details to be conscious of while implementing a persistent storage cache, but the benefits (offline access, faster start-up times, fewer app-halting loading dialogs) make it more than worth your effort.

THE FETCH

Now that you've got a place to save images as you download them, it's time to implement the image fetcher. Here's the handleIntent method:

```
protected void onHandleIntent(Intent intent) {
    String remoteUrl = intent.getExtras().getString("url");
    String location;
    String filename =
        remoteUrl.substring(
        remoteUrl.lastIndexOf(File.separator)+1);
    File tmp = new File(cacheDir.getPath()
            + File.separator +filename);
    if(tmp.exists()){
        location = tmp.getAbsolutePath();
        notifyFinished(location, remoteUrl);
```

```
            stopSelf();
            return;
        }
        try{
            URL url = new URL(remoteUrl);
            HttpURLConnection httpCon =
                (HttpURLConnection)url.openConnection();
            if(httpCon.getResponseCode() != 200)
                throw new Exception("Failed to connect");
            InputStream is = httpCon.getInputStream();
            FileOutputStream fos = new FileOutputStream(tmp);
            writeStream(is, fos);
            fos.flush(); fos.close();
            is.close();
            location = tmp.getAbsolutePath();
            notifyFinished(location, remoteUrl);
        }catch(Exception e){
            Log.e("Service","Failed!",e);
        }
    }
```

This is a lot of code. Fortunately, most of it is stuff you've seen before.

First, you retrieve the URL to be downloaded from the Extras bundle on the intent. Next, you determine a cache file name by taking the last part of the URL. Once you know what the file will eventually be called, you can check to see if it's already in the cache. If it is, you're finished, and you can notify the system that the image is available to load into the UI.

If the file isn't cached, you'll need to download it. By now you've seen the HttpUrlConnection code used to download an image at least once, so I won't bore you by covering it. Also, if you've written any Java code before, you probably know how to write an input stream to disk.

THE CLEANUP

At this point, you've created the cache file, retrieved it from the web, and written it to the aforementioned cache file. It's time to notify anyone who might be listening that the image is available. Here's the contents of the notifyFinished method that will tell the system both that the image is finished and where to get it.

```
public static final String TRANSACTION_DONE =
                    "com.haseman.TRANSACTION_DONE";
private void notifyFinished(String location, String remoteUrl){
    Intent i = new Intent(TRANSACTION_DONE);
    i.putExtra("location", location);
    i.putExtra("url", remoteUrl);
    ImageIntentService.this.sendBroadcast(i);
}
```

Anyone listening for the broadcast intent com.haseman.TRANSACTION_DONE will be notified that an image download has finished. They will be able to pull both the URL (so they can tell if it was an image it actually requested) and the location of the cached file.

RENDERING THE DOWNLOAD

In order to interact with the downloading service, there are two steps you'll need to take. You'll need to start the service (with the URL you want it to fetch). Before it starts, however, you'll need to register a listener for the result broadcast. You can see these two steps in the following code:

```
public void onCreate(Bundle extras){
    super.onCreate(extras);
    setContentView(R.layout.image_layout);
    IntentFilter intentFilter = new IntentFilter();
        intentFilter.addAction(ImageIntentService.TRANSACTION_DONE);
    registerReceiver(imageReceiver, intentFilter);
```

```
    Intent i = new Intent(this, ImageIntentService.class);
    i.putExtra("url",
getIntent().getExtras().getString("url"));
    startService(i);
    pd = ProgressDialog.show(this, "Fetching Image",
"Go intent service go!");
}
```

This code registered a receiver (so you can take action once the download is finished), started the service, and, finally, showed a loading dialog to the user.

Now take a look at what the imageReceiver class looks like:

```
private BroadcastReceiver imageReceiver = new BroadcastReceiver() {
@Override
    public void onReceive(Context context, Intent intent) {
        String location = intent.getExtras().getString("location");
        if(location == null || location.length() ==0){
            Toast.makeText(context, "Failed to download image",
                    Toast.LENGTH_LONG).show();
        }
        File imageFile = new File(location);
        if(!imageFile.exists()){
            pd.dismiss();
            Toast.makeText(context,
                "Unable to Download file :-(",
                Toast.LENGTH_LONG);
            return;
        }
        Bitmap b = BitmapFactory.decodeFile(location);
```

```
            ImageView iv = (ImageView)findViewById(R.id.remote_image);
            iv.setImageBitmap(b);
            pd.dismiss();
        }
    };
```

This is a custom extension of the `BroadcastReceiver` class. This is what you'll need to declare inside your activity in order to correctly process events from the `IntentService`. Right now, there are two problems with this code. See if you can recognize them.

First, you'll need to extract the file location from the intent. You do this by looking for the "location" extra. Once you've verified that this is indeed a valid file, you'll pass it over to the `BitmapFactory`, which will create the image for you. This bitmap can then be passed off to the `ImageView` for rendering.

Now, to the things done wrong (stop reading if you haven't found them yet. No cheating!). First, the code is not checking to see if the intent service is broadcasting a completion intent for exactly the image originally asked for (keep in mind that one service can service requests from any number of activities).

Second, the bitmap is loading from the SD card…on the main thread! Exactly one of the things I've been warning you NOT to do.

CHECKING YOUR WORK

Android, in later versions of the SDK tools, has provided a way to check if your application is breaking the rules and running slow tasks on the main thread. You can, in any activity, call `StrictMode.enableDefaults`, and this will begin to throw warnings when the system spots main thread violations. `StrictMode` has many different configurations and settings, but enabling the defaults and cleaning up as many errors as you can will work wonders for the speed of your application.

THE **LOADER**

Loader is a new class that comes both in Honeycomb and in the Android Compatibility library. Sadly, there is not enough space in this chapter to cover it in detail, but I will say that it's an excellent tool to explore if you must do heavy lifting off the main thread repeatedly. It, like AsyncTask, is usually bound to an activity, but it is much better suited to handle situations where a single task must be performed many times. It's great for loading cursors (with the CursorLoader subclass) and for other tasks, like downloading individual list items for a ListView. Check the documentation for how best to use this new and powerful class.

WRAPPING **UP**

That about covers us on how to load data. Remember, loading from the SD card, network transactions, and longer processing tasks MUST be performed off the main thread, or your application, and users, will suffer. You can, as I've shown you in this chapter, use a simple thread, an AsyncTask, or an IntentService to retrieve and process your data. But remember, too, that any action modifying any view or object onscreen must be carried out on the main thread (or Android will throw angry exceptions at you).

Further, keep in mind that these three methods are only a few of many possible background data fetching patterns. Loaders, Workers, and ThreadPools are all other alternatives that might suit your application better than the examples I've given.

Follow the simple rules I've outlined here, and your app will be fast, it will be responsive to your users, and it will avoid the dreaded App Not Responding notification of doom. Correct use and avoidance of the main thread is critical to producing a successful application.

If you're more interested in building lists out of complex data from remote sources, the next chapter should give you exactly what you're looking for. I'll be showing you how to render a list of Twitter messages to a menu onscreen.

I'll leave you with a final challenge: Enable Android's strict mode and move the little file accesses I've left in this chapter's sample code off the main thread. It should be a good way to familiarize yourself with the process before you undertake it on your own.

5

ADAPTERS, LISTVIEWS, AND LISTS

Lists, in Android, are one of the most often-used tools to show data to users. From the entry menu of a game to a dynamic list of Facebook statuses or Twitter messages, lists are everywhere. Android's system for dealing with them, while complicated at first, becomes much easier once you begin using it. In this chapter, I'll run the gamut from simple, static main-menu lists to the dynamic, remote-data-backed custom list elements of a Twitter feed. Along the way, I'll expose you to the inner workings of one of Android's most often-used and complex UI views.

TWO **PIECES** TO **EACH LIST**

To display lists of ordered data with Android, there are two major components you'll need to deal with.

LISTVIEW

First, you'll need a ListView in which to display your content. This is the view whose job it is to display the information. It can be added to any screen layout, or you can use Android's ListActivity or ListFragment to handle some of the organization for you. If your screen is primarily designed to show a collection of data to the user in list form, I highly suggest you use ListActivity and its cousin ListFragment.

ADAPTER

The second major class you'll need to deal with is the Adapter. This is the object that will feed the individual views, a little bit at a time, to the ListView. It's also responsible for filling and configuring the individual rows to be populated in the ListView. There are as many Adapter subclasses as drops of water in the ocean (all right, perhaps slightly fewer), and they cover the range of data types—from static string lists (ArrayAdapters) to the more dynamic lists (CursorAdapters). You can extend your own adapter (which I'll show you in the second half of this chapter). For now, let me show you how to create a simple main menu with a ListView.

As always, you can either follow along with the sample code I've posted at Peachpit.com/androiddevelopanddesign or open your IDE and do the tasks I've outlined.

A MAIN MENU

Main menus can take any number of forms. From games to music apps, they provide a top-level navigation into the app as a whole.

They are also, as a happy side effect, a great way to introduce you to how lists work. I'll be creating an array of strings for the resource manager, feeding it to an array adapter, and plugging that array adapter into the list view contained by a list activity. Got all that? There are a lot of moving parts to collect when dealing with lists, so I'll take it slowly and step by step.

CREATING THE MENU DATA

A menu must have something to display, so you need to create a list of strings to be displayed. Remember the chapter where you learned that all displayed string constants *should* go into the res/values/strings.xml file? String arrays, coincidentally, go into the same file, but with a slightly different syntax. I've added the following to my res/values/strings.xml file:

```
<?xml version="1.0" encoding="utf-8"?>

<resources>

    <!--The rest of the app's strings here-->

    <string name="app_name">List Example</string>

    <string name="main_menu">Main Menu</string>

<string-array name="menu_entries">

        <item>Menu Item One</item>

        <item>Menu Item Two</item>

        <item>Menu Item Three</item>

    </string-array>

</resources>
```

Instead of defining each constant inside a string tag, this time you'll declare a string array with a name, and then each element within it can be defined inside an item tag. Now that you have data, it's time to create an activity in which to house it.

CREATING A LISTACTIVITY

Now you need a place to display your items. You'll create an instance of `ListActivity` in which to display your recently created list.

Every screen must have an activity, and list screens are no exception. In this case, Android provides you a helper class that was built specifically to make list screens easier. It's called the `ListActivity`, and it behaves exactly like an activity does except that it has a few extra methods to make life easier. If you're coding along with the chapter, you'll need to create a new project. Take the main activity you'd normally have, and modify it to look like the following listing:

```
package com.haseman.lists;
import android.app.ListActivity;
import android.os.Bundle;
public class MainMenuActivity extends ListActivity{
    public void onCreate(Bundle bundle){
        super.onCreate(bundle);
        setContentView(R.layout.list_activity);
    }
}
```

This code will not, however, compile at the moment, because I haven't yet defined what `R.layout.list_activity` looks like. Guess what you're going to do next?

DEFINING A LAYOUT FOR YOUR LISTACTIVITY

You will need to create an XML layout file for your list. Again, this is similar to other layout tasks you've done, with one notable exception: You need to define a `ListView` with the special ID `android:id/list`. This is what tells the system which list view is the main list view your new `ListActivity` will interact with. I've also added a `TextView` to the layout as a large title. My XML file looks like the following:

```xml
<?xml version="1.0" encoding="utf-8"?>
<LinearLayout
    xmlns:android="http://schemas.android.com/apk/res/android"
    android:layout_width="match_parent"
    android:layout_height="match_parent"
    android:orientation="vertical">
        <TextView
        android:layout_width="match_parent"
        android:layout_height="0dp"
        android:layout_weight="1"
        android:text="@string/main_menu"
        android:gravity="center"
        android:textSize="40dp"/>
    <ListView
        android:id="@android:id/list"
        android:layout_width="fill_parent"
        android:layout_height="0dp"
        android:layout_weight="1"
    android:gravity="center"/>
</LinearLayout>
```

TIP: Special IDs: You only need to call the `android:id/list` `ListView` if you're using the built-in convenience methods of `ListActivity`. If you're using a regular activity, you can use any ID you want. This special ID is what connects the `ListActivity` to the single `ListView` with which it is going to interact.

This XML layout code should look familiar to you, given what you've read in
previous chapters. It's simply splitting the screen space between the title main
menu and the list of sub-screens. You can also see the special Android list ID that
is needed to tell the ListActivity which view it should interact with.

MAKING A MENU LIST ITEM

Now you'll create a layout XML file for the individual list element.

You'll need to declare a separate layout object to define how each element
will look in the list. I'm using a very simple version of the ArrayAdapter, so at
this point, the layout XML file *must* contain only a single text view. We'll get into
more-complex menu items later in the chapter.

Next, you'll need to create a new file, containing a single text view, in the /res/
layout/ folder. Here's what /res/layout/list_element.xml looks like in my project:

```xml
<?xml version="1.0" encoding="utf-8"?>

<TextView

    xmlns:android="http://schemas.android.com/apk/res/android"

    android:gravity="center"

    android:layout_height="wrap_content"

    android:layout_width="match_parent"

    android:textSize="20dp"

    android:padding="15dp"/>
```

You don't actually need to supply an ID for this text view, because you'll be referencing it in its capacity as a layout object (R.layout.list_element, in this case). Setting the gravity to center tells the view that you want the text to lie in the center of the extra available space. Setting the padding to 15dp will also give the views a little bit of extra space, so people with hands like mine can hit the correct one.

Now that I've declared what I want the list elements to look like, I can go about adding them to the ListView itself.

CREATING AND POPULATING THE ARRAYADAPTER

Create and configure an ArrayAdapter. The ArrayAdapter will communicate your data to the ListView. It will also inflate however many copies of the list_element layout are needed to keep the ListView full of data. As a last step, here's what you'll need to add to the MainMenuActivity's onCreate method:

```
public void onCreate(Bundle bundle){

super.onCreate(bundle);

    setContentView(R.layout.list_activity);

    ArrayAdapter<CharSequence> adapter =

        ArrayAdapter.createFromResource(getApplicationContext(),

        R.array.menu_entries, R.layout.list_element);

    setListAdapter(adapter);

}
```

Because the ListView has the special @android:id/list system ID, the List Activity knows where to find the ListView. As a result, you'll only have to create the adapter and hand it over to the ListActivity. The ListActivity will make sure that it's correctly plugged into the ListView and that everything is drawn correctly.

FIGURE 5.1 A very basic main menu.

To create the ArrayAdapter, I specify the array of strings I defined in the section "Creating the Menu Data" as well as the list_element layout I created in "Making a Menu List Item." Assuming that all your Tab A's are correctly fitted into your Slot B's, the resulting screen will look something like **Figure 5.1**.

Do a little dance—you've now got a functional (albeit very simple) list! Have a smoke, cup of coffee, sip of wine, or dog treat. Whatever you do to reward yourself for a job well done, do it now. I'll be here when you get back.

REACTING TO CLICK EVENTS

Your code will need to listen for item clicks.

What's the point of having a menu if you can't tell when items have been selected? Right, there isn't one. Let me show you the final piece to my basic list menu example. Add the following method to your MainMenuActivity.java file:

```
@Override
public void onListItemClick(ListView lv,
    View clickedView,
    int position, long id)
{
    super.onListItemClick(lv, clickedView, position, id);
    TextView tv = (TextView)clickedView;
    Toast.makeText(getApplicationContext(),
        "List Item "+tv.getText()+" was clicked!",
        Toast.LENGTH_SHORT).show();
}
```

The ListActivity will call this method (if you've defined it) every time an element in the list view is clicked (or tapped with a finger). For more-complicated lists, you may want to use the ID (especially if you are using SQLite as a backing store). For this simple demo, I've just popped up a little dialog showing the text of the item that was pressed. If you're implementing your own basic main menu, I suggest you use the position of the clicked item to start an activity, service, or other action. You can see an example of this if you look at the associated source code.

That's the most basic list view I could possibly show you. Now, I'll take you in the opposite direction and show you what a custom list backed by a remote data source looks like.

COMPLEX LIST VIEWS

While building a main menu is great and all, there are much more complicated uses to which you can put the Adapter and ListView combination. In fact, I'm going to show you an example that gets complicated in two ways. First, the data source is going to be from a remote URL (a Twitter feed). Second, I'm going to add a second text view to the list (you could, if you want to, add any number of items to it).

THE 1000-FOOT VIEW

All right, here's the game plan. First, you'll need an AsyncTask to retrieve the feed from Twitter's API. Once you have the data, you'll need to parse it into JSON (JavaScript Object Notation) objects and feed that data into a custom adapter. Last, you'll need to create that custom adapter and the specific ListView layout to hold the two pieces of text info. With those things in hand, you can create the custom layout object.

In the end, you'll have a list of Peachpit's 20 most recent Twitter messages, along with when they were written. If a message was retweeted, the text will display in red. This is by no means the most complex list you could build using these tools, but it is a great way to show you how to make your own complex custom list views.

CREATING THE MAIN LAYOUT VIEW

This step is very similar to the "Defining a Layout for Your ListActivity" section. You'll need an XML layout containing a ListView with the android:id/list ID. In this case, however, because the data isn't available when the activity launches, you'll need the ListView to start out hidden. Here's what my project's XML layout looks like:

```xml
<?xml version="1.0" encoding="utf-8"?>

<LinearLayout xmlns:android="http://schemas.android.com/apk/
    res/android"

    android:orientation="vertical"

    android:layout_width="match_parent"

    android:layout_height="match_parent">

    <TextView

    android:id="@+id/loading_text"

    android:layout_width="match_parent"

    android:layout_height="wrap_content"
```

```
    android:text="@string/loading"

    android:gravity="center"/>

    <ListView

    android:id="@android:id/list"

    android:layout_width="match_parent"

    android:layout_height="match_parent"

    android:visibility="gone"/>

</LinearLayout>
```

CREATING THE LISTACTIVITY

Again, you're going to need a new ListActivity. Since you're already good at getting them started, I'll just skip to showing you what my onCreate method looks like:

```
private TwitterAsyncTask twitterFetcher;

@Override

public void onCreate(Bundle savedInstanceState) {

    super.onCreate(savedInstanceState);

    setContentView(R.layout.main);

    Adapter adapter = new TwitterJSONAdapter();

    setListAdapter(adapter);

    twitterFetcher = new TwitterAsyncTask();

        twitterFetcher.execute("https://api.twitter.com/1/statuses/
    →  user_timeline.json?include_entities=false&include_
    →  rts=false&screen_name=peachpit&count=20");

}
```

> **NOTE:** If the Twitter URL in the earlier code listing isn't working, I've stashed a backup copy of the data at http://wanderingoak.net/ twitter_backup.json. If Twitter changes their API, you can always run the sample code against that URL.

This method call does two things of note. First, it creates a new custom Twitter JSONAdapter, which I'll show you how to create in a minute. Second, it creates a TwitterAsyncTask and fires it off.

You'll have noticed, if you were watching closely, that I created a private data member to contain the Twitter-fetching task. You astute readers might be wondering why I chose to stash it aside that way. The answer is that because this task isn't happening on the main thread, I need to be able to cancel it should the user close down the activity before the task finishes. To do this, the onStop method will need to be able to call the Twitter-fetching AsyncTask, making it a private data member.

GETTING TWITTER DATA

My first task, at least when it comes to doing work, is to load the stream of Twitter messages. You should, thanks to the previous chapter, be very familiar with the ins and outs of fetching network data. Thanks to your amazing proficiency, I'm going to hide the code required to do a network call and read it into a string. If you're having trouble remembering how to do this, feel free to check out the sample code.

Without further preamble, here's what my TwitterAsyncTask looks like:

```
private class TwitterAsyncTask extends
    AsyncTask<String, Integer, JSONArray>{
    @Override
    protected JSONArray doInBackground(String... params) {
        String response = getURLContents(params[0]);
        try {
            return new JSONArray(response);
        } catch (JSONException ex) { return null; }
    }
```

```java
@Override
protected void onPostExecute(JSONArray response){
    if(response == null)
        return;
    try{
        ((TwitterJSONAdapter)getListAdapter())
.setData(response);
        getListView().setVisibility(View.VISIBLE);
        View loading = findViewById(R.id.loading_text);
        if(loading!=null)
            loading.setVisibility(View.GONE);
    }catch(Exception e){
        Log.e("TwitterFeed","Failed to set Adapter");
    }
    }
}
```

HANDLING **EXCEPTIONS**

It's *always* a good idea to print out the cause of any particular exception when it's caught. This is, at its core, just Java best practices. If an exception comes through and you're not printing it to Android's LogCat tool, things can get very confusing, very fast. When beginners have trouble debugging a problem, it's often because they're catching and releasing exceptions that contain important information.

Again, if you're struggling with how to fetch the data at the end of a URL and turn that data into a string full of JSON, check the included sample code for the contents of getTwitterFeed. Here are the general steps for fetching the data:

1. Create a JSON array from the string that was fed back to you in getTwitter Feed. This will parse the data, which you then return at the end of the doInBackground method.

2. Once you're back on the main thread inside the onPostExecute method, it's time to pass the JSON array to the custom adapter (which I promise to show you in just a second). Updating the data will trigger a redraw of the list view.

3. Hide the initial "Loading..." TextView that I defined in the XML layout file, and show the list instead.

NOTE: Any changes to the Adapter's data must take place on the main thread. Modifying the Adapter data counts as changing the UI, as far as Android is concerned. As always, all changes to the user interface must be carried out on the main thread. Keep this is mind as you create your own adapter, especially if you're fetching data from the network off the main thread.

MAKING A CUSTOM ADAPTER

All right, now comes the really interesting part. You need to create a custom Adapter to feed rows into the ListView.

Custom Adapters have four methods you are required to override, all of which allow the ListView to acquire information about your data set.

- getCount() returns the number of rows currently in the set of information.

- getItem(int position) returns an object corresponding to a particular row position.

- getItemId(int position) returns the ID that corresponds to the item at a specific position. This is used often with Adapters that focus on Cursors (Android's SQLite interfaces).

- getView(int position, View convertView, ViewGroup parent) is where most of the Adapter's work will take place. The ListView, in making this call, is essentially asking for the view at position. You must, in this method, return a correctly configured view for the data at position. More on exactly how this works in a minute.

As you can see by the get prefix on all the required methods, all that Android Adapters do is provide row content information to the ListView. The ListView, it would seem, is one very needy girlfriend (or boyfriend...I'm not sure how to assign gender to Android UI interfaces).

Let me show you the example before I talk about any more theory. Twitter's API returns its information in the form of JSON-encoded objects. It doesn't, at this point, make sense to translate it to some other data store, so I'll design my custom adapter to use a JSONArray object as its data backer. This class is declared as an inner class definition in ListActivity.

```
private class TwitterJSONAdapter extends BaseAdapter {
    JSONArray data;
    //Must be called on the main thread
    private void setData(JSONArray data){
        this.data = data;
        this.notifyDataSetChanged();
    }
    @Override
    public int getCount() {
        if(data==null)
            return 0;
        else
            return data.length();
    }
```

```
@Override
public Object getItem(int position) {
    if(data==null)
        return null;
    try{
        JSONObject element = (JSONObject)data.get(position);
        return element;
    }catch(Exception e){
        return null;
    }
}
@Override
public long getItemId(int position) {
    return position;
}
```

This code, for the most part, wraps accessors to the JSON object. It handles getting an item from a position (which in this example is the index into the JSON array). If no data has been set, then the Adapter simply reports that there's nothing to see. The only method in the example that doesn't override a required function is the code that changes the data set. It also calls notifyDataSetChanged and, as a result of this method, must be called on the main thread. My class extends from BaseAdapter because it contains all the baseline methods that I need to build my custom adapter.

BUILDING THE LISTVIEWS

At last you've come to the part where you get to build and return the individual custom list view elements. Here's the code to do exactly that:

```
@Override
public View getView(int position, View convertView,
    ViewGroup parent) {
    JSONObject node = (JSONObject)getItem(position);
    ViewGroup listView = null;
    //Reduce, Reuse, Recycle!
    if(convertView == null)
        listView =
        (ViewGroup)getLayoutInflater().inflate
            (R.layout.twitter_list_item, null);
    else
        listView = (ViewGroup)convertView;
    try{
        boolean retweeted = node.getInt("retweet_count") > 0;
        TextView tv =
        (TextView)listView.findViewById(R.id.text_one);
        tv.setText(node.getString("text"));
        if(retweeted)
            tv.setTextColor(0xFFFF0000);
        else
            tv.setTextColor(0xFFFFFFFF);
        tv = (TextView)listView.findViewById(R.id.text_two);
        tv.setText(node.getString("created_at"));
```

```
                    if(retweeted)
                        tv.setTextColor(0xFFFF0000);
                    else
                        tv.setTextColor(0xFFFFFFFF);
            }catch(JSONException e){
                Log.e("TwitterView","Failed to set list item",e);
            }
    return listView;
    }
```

There are a couple of key points to consider in the getView code listing.

First, you need to figure out if the view can be recycled. If it can, you'll reset *all* the visible values for it; otherwise, you'll inflate a new row—by using the Layout Inflater—and configure it (more on how and why this works soon).

Second, you'll detect, from the JSONObject, if the message has been retweeted by checking the retweet count. If it has, you'll set the text color for both text views.

Last, you'll pull both the text and created_at strings from the JSONObject and set them as the two text views. You might have noticed that I haven't shown you what twitter_list_item.xml looks like. That is the view layout I'm creating (by calling the inflate method and passing in the layout).

THE CUSTOM LAYOUT VIEW

This layout has just two TextViews in it, with the very original IDs of text_one and text_two and can be found in res/layout/twitter_list_item:

```xml
<?xml version="1.0" encoding="utf-8"?>
<LinearLayout
    xmlns:android="http://schemas.android.com/apk/res/android"
    android:orientation="vertical"
    android:layout_width="match_parent"
    android:layout_height="match_parent">
    <TextView
```

```
    android:id="@+id/text_one"

    android:layout_width="match_parent"

    android:layout_height="wrap_content"

    android:padding="6dp"/>

<TextView

    android:id="@+id/text_two"

    android:layout_width="match_parent"

    android:layout_height="wrap_content"

    android:padding="6dp"/>

</LinearLayout>
```

With this layout, you now have all the moving pieces you need to download, parse, and display a Twitter feed. **Figure 5.2**, at last, is what Peachpit's Twitter feed looks like in ListView form.

HOW DO THESE OBJECTS INTERACT?

To understand how the ListView interacts with the Adapter, there are a few constraints you must understand. First, lists could scroll on to infinity, at least from the point of view of the device. Yet, as you might have guessed, the phone has a limited amount of memory. This means that not every single list item can have its own entry in the list, because the device would quickly run out of space. Further, if the ListView had to lay out every single row right up front, it could be bogged down for an unacceptable amount of time.

What Android does to solve these problems is to recycle list element rows. The process looks a little bit like this:

1. Android goes through the entire list, asking each row how large it would like to be (this is so it knows how large to draw the scroll indicator).

2. Once it knows roughly how big the entire ListView will be, it then requests views for the first screen, plus a buffer (so it won't have to stop and get more when the user starts scrolling). Your adapter will have to create, configure, and return those views as the ListView calls getView over and over again.

3. As the user scrolls down and rows fall off the top of the list, Android will return them to you when it calls getView. Effectively, it's asking you to reuse a previous view by passing in the convertView object to you.

While recycling list element rows is great for conserving memory and speeding up long lists, it has some interesting side effects.

- All your list views, in order to take advantage of the built-in recycling, must always inflate from the same row layout. Android won't know what type of list item you'll want to create; so if you had, for example, three different row layouts, the system would not know which one to pass back to you, and you'd have to handle your own pools of unused views.

- Any asynchronous task, such as loading an icon from disk or loading a user's profile icon, must check that the ListView hasn't recycled the view while it's been downloading or loading the image data. If the row is still showing the same data when the task finishes, it's safe to update the row; otherwise, it needs to cache or chuck the data.

WRAPPING **UP**

This chapter covered the basics of both simple and custom ListViews and Adapters. I showed you how to create a simple main menu, and I walked you through a simple example of building a custom Adapter to handle a more complex ListView. You now have a grasp of the basics.

Lists are still one of the cornerstones of mobile development. I advise you, however, to make as few boring, graphically flat lists as you possibly can. While these examples are great for showing you how to build lists of your own, they are by no means shining examples of solid interface design. You can, and very much should, make lists when needed, but dress them up as much as you can without affecting performance.

If you're hungering for more, I highly suggest reading through Android's implementation of ListActivity.java. Because Android is open source, you can get all the code that makes up its SDK for free! Head over to http://source.android.com for more information.

Lastly, I wrote more code for this chapter than I had space to explain here. I recommend checking out the sample code associated with this chapter (at Peachpit.com/androiddevelopanddesign) to learn more about launching a screen as the result of a menu click and about how to build a similar main menu screen using a ListFragment.

6

THE **WAY** OF THE **SERVICE**

Services are one of the most important, and often under-utilized, components of the Android platform. They are essential for accomplishing any task whose data or relevance can span more than one activity. They are like activities in that they have a lifecycle (albeit a much simpler one), but they do not have the activity's ability to draw to the screen. In practice, services break down into two major use cases: the listener and the task. Listeners are services that hang out in the background, waiting for something to happen that prompts them to take action. Task services are akin to the photo downloader that we covered before, so in this chapter I'll focus on listening services.

WHAT IS A SERVICE?

A Service is, at its most basic level, a class with a simple runtime lifecycle and no access to the screen. You had some contact with the IntentService back in Chapter 4 when I showed you how to retrieve an image with it, but I now have the chance to help you really dig into this simple yet powerful component.

Keep in mind that while the service might be important to *you*, it is not more important to Android than the smooth running of the overall device. This means that at any point the system may shut down your service if it determines that it's been running too long, that it's been consuming too many resources, or that it's the third Friday of the month and there's a full moon. There is a way to tell the system not to kill you off, and I'll show what that looks like in just a second.

THE SERVICE LIFECYCLE

A service is, essentially, a singleton. Any component in your application may call startService with an intent that specifies the service they want to get running. If the service isn't running, Android will initialize a new one; otherwise, it will just notify the existing one that a new start command has been issued. Here's a brief rundown of the service's lifecycle.

- onCreate is called on the main thread when the service is started up. It's a good time to initialize any data you're going to rely on throughout the run of the service.

- onStartCommand will be called every time an activity (or any other component) calls startService. The intent passed into startService will be handed off to your onStartCommand call.

- onBind is your chance to return, to the caller, an interface object that allows direct method calls on the service. The binder, however, is optional and only really needed for a heavy level of communication with your service. This results in a different method of interaction than calling Context.startService. Like startService, bindService takes an intent and will start up the service if it's not already running. If absolutely none of what I just wrote makes sense, that's fine; it'll make much more sense to you by the end of the chapter.

At this point in the lifecycle, your service is now happily running along. Music can be played, data can be acquired (remember the main thread!), and recordings can be made and crunched for voice commands.

Just because you're running in a service doesn't mean you're off the main thread! The service's onCreate method *will* be called on the main thread. If you need to do any heavy lifting, consider using an AsyncTask or a Handler+Looper pattern, or instead of doing a normal service, use an IntentService to process heavy data off the main thread. Further, there are certain actions (like recording audio) that you can initiate only from the main thread. It's 10 a.m., do you know where your threads are?

KEEPING YOUR SERVICE RUNNING

The startForeground method is your chance to strike a clever deal with Android. The system agrees that after you call this method and until you call stopForeground, it will not kill off your service. In exchange, you must provide an icon and view to be shown to the user in the top bar by handing it a Notification object. This contract allows long-running, essential, and intensive services (such as music playback or photo uploading) to run without fear of extermination. At the same time, the user is aware of why their phone might be a little sluggish.

SHUT IT DOWN!

At some point, the party will end and it'll be time to clean up. This can happen because your service called stopSelf or because another component called Context.stopService. Here's the teardown portion of the lifecycle:

- onDestroy is your chance to cancel any running tasks and put away any resource you've taken on (for example, media or network tasks). This is also your chance to unregister any BroadcastReceivers or ContentObservers that you've set up to watch for new media.

If you were expecting a many-step shutdown process, I'm afraid you're going to be disappointed. Because services have no notion of being on top of the screen, there is no need to pause, resume, or do any of the other complex interactions that activities must support.

COMMUNICATION

There are two main ways to communicate with a service: intent broadcasts and binder interfaces. I'm going to show you examples of both and, along the way, let you see two practical tasks for a service. There are, in fact, many more ways you can communicate with your services. But in my experience, these are the two most useful. As always, check the documentation if neither of these approaches feels quite right for you.

INTENT-BASED COMMUNICATION

Imagine two workers in different rooms who can only communicate with each other by email. These emails can contain attachments and other pieces of data. The two workers must get through their day using only this one method of communication. As you might imagine, this can be an efficient and functional way to get a multitude of things done, as long as they don't have to say too much to each other.

This is, in a sense, exactly what *intent-based communication* with services would look like translated to real life. The service is started with an intent; when it completes its task or something that it's waiting for occurs, it sends a broadcast intent alerting anyone listening that a particular task is finished. You saw one example of this in Chapter 4 when I was downloading images using an intent service. Let me show you one more.

The following example is one of the best examples of intent-based communication that I can give you in this printed form. I'll create all the pieces required for a new service that runs, with a notification, in the foreground. I use Android's ContentProvider to listen for and acquire the location of new photographs as they are taken. This code will alert you when any new picture is snapped, regardless of the application used to do it. What you do with the photograph, I'll leave to your boundless imagination.

AUTO IMAGE UPLOADING

One of my favorite features of the Google+ Android app is its ability to automatically upload photos in the background. It turns out that with a ContentProvider, Service, and ContentObserver, you can do this quite easily in your own app. My sample service will launch, place itself in the foreground, and trigger a broadcast intent whenever a new photo is taken. You could, in your own code, upload the image or take any number of other actions. Using this technique would involve the following general steps.

1. Declare the service.

2. Get yourself a service.

3. Start the service.

4. Spin up the service.

5. Go to the foreground.

6. Observe when content changes.

Let's get started.

DECLARING THE SERVICE

You must tell Android where to find the service.

Each service, as you know, must be declared in the manifest. You can add an intent filter for it to respond to (if you want applications other than your own to be able to start it). For my example, this isn't necessary, but it might be something you need to take advantage of later. Here's the single line you'll need to place in your manifest:

```
<service android:name="PhotoListenerService"/>
```

GETTING YOURSELF A SERVICE

Now create the class that extends service.

```
public class PhotoListenerService extends Service {
    @Override
    public IBinder onBind(Intent intent) {
        return null;
    }
}
```

Since onBind is a required method for the Service class, it has to be in my class or it won't compile. Now that you've got a service, let's look at how to actually start it.

STARTING THE SERVICE

Start the service from your activity. When I created the project, I got a default activity (I named mine, quite originally, ServiceExampleActivity) and a main.xml view.

1. Modify that view to contain Start and Stop buttons, like so:

```xml
<?xml version="1.0" encoding="utf-8"?>
<LinearLayout xmlns:android="http://schemas.android.com/
    apk/res/android"
    android:orientation="vertical"
    android:layout_width="match_parent"
    android:layout_height="match_parent"
    >
    <Button
    android:id="@+id/start_service"
        android:layout_width="wrap_content"
        android:layout_height="wrap_content"
        android:text="start service"
        android:padding="15dp"
        android:gravity="center"/>
    <Button
    android:id="@+id/stop_service"
        android:layout_width="wrap_content"
        android:layout_height="wrap_content"
        android:text="stop service"
        android:padding="15dp"
        android:gravity="center"/>
</LinearLayout>
```

The buttons are a simple way to put some clickable text on the screen.

2. With these in place, you can now write code to start and stop the photo listening service. Here's what the updated ServiceExampleActivity now looks like:

```
public class ServiceExampleActivity extends Activity
            implements OnClickListener{
    /** Called when the activity is first created. */
    @Override
    public void onCreate(Bundle savedInstanceState) {
        super.onCreate(savedInstanceState);
        setContentView(R.layout.main);
        Button btn = (Button)findViewById(R.id.start_service);
        btn.setOnClickListener(this);
        btn = (Button)findViewById(R.id.stop_service);
        btn.setOnClickListener(this);
    }
}
```

Nothing earth-shattering in this listing. I'm retrieving references to the views once they've been built. I set my class to implement the OnClickListener interface, which allows me to set the activity itself as the click listener for the two buttons. The above code will not compile until you implement View.onClick.

3. Implement the onClick method:

```
@Override
public void onClick(View v) {
    Intent serviceIntent = new Intent(getApplicationContext(),
                    PhotoListenerService.class);
    if(v.getId() == R.id.start_service){
```

```
            startService(serviceIntent);
        }
        else if(v.getId() == R.id.stop_service){
            stopService(serviceIntent);
        }
    }
```

This, again, is pretty simple. The buttons, when clicked, will call this onClick method. Depending on the view that actually got the click, I'll either start or stop the service.

SPINNING UP THE SERVICE
Right now, if you were to run the code as it stands, you'd press the button, the service would start, and...nothing whatsoever would happen. Let me show you how to change that.

I want to be notified by the system every time someone takes a picture with the device's camera. To do this, you'll have to register an observer with Android's media ContentProvider. Switching back to the PhotoListenerService.java file, register for media notifications in the service's onCreate method:

```
@Override
public void onCreate(){
    super.onCreate();
    getContentResolver().
    registerContentObserver(
        MediaStore.Images.Media.EXTERNAL_CONTENT_URI,
        true,
        observer);
}
```

To register a content observer, I'll need to provide a Uniform Resource Identifier (URI). In this case, I'll use the constant URI for all photos saved on the external SD card. This constant is declared in the MediaStore. The second parameter is me telling Android that I'd like to know when children of that URI are modified. I set it to true because I'll want to know when any of the descendants of the image URI are modified, added, or deleted. Last, I pass in my observer. This is the object whose onChange method will be called whenever the ContentProvider is updated. It will register for media updates, but there's still one more method you'll need to define.

GOING TO THE FOREGROUND

Bringing your service into the foreground protects it from being killed by Android when resources are low.

Implement the onStartCommand method of your service as follows.

```
public int onStartCommand(Intent intent, int flags, int startId) {
    super.onStartCommand(intent, flags, startId);
    lastUpdateTime = System.currentTimeMillis();
    setForegroundState(true);
    return Service.START_STICKY;
}
```

I'm going to record when the service started (more on why that's important in just a second). Last, I return Service.START_STICKY, which tells the system that, should the service be terminated for memory or performance reasons, I'd like to have it started back up.

I need to write a function to handle creating a notification and moving the service into the foreground. setForegroundState is my own method that handles placing the service and removing the service from foreground mode.

```
private void setForegroundState(boolean enable){
    if(enable){
        Notification n = new Notification(
            R.drawable.icon,
            "Service Is uploading all your photos",
                System.currentTimeMillis());
        n.contentView = new RemoteViews(
```

```
                    "com.haseman.serviceExample",
                    R.layout.notification);
                Intent clickIntent = new Intent(
                    getApplicationContext(),
                    ServiceExampleActivity.class);
                n.contentIntent =
                    PendingIntent.getActivity(
                    getApplicationContext(), 0, clickIntent , 0);
                startForeground(1, n);
            }
            else{
                stopForeground(true);
            }
        }
```

Thanks to the wonders of line wrapping, this code is a little tricky to read. Essentially, in order to go into foreground mode, you need at the very least a Notification object, a RemoteView, and an intent that fires when the user clicks the pull-down notification. Let me break it down a little more.

Start by creating a Notification object, which requires three things:

- A small icon resource, to be constantly displayed along the top of the notification bar.

- A string, to be briefly flashed along the top bar when the notification appears.

- The time at which to display the notification (in this case, right now!). This constructor returns a Notification object to which you can add the rest of the required objects.

You'll next see me create a RemoteView for the pull-down notification bar and set it in the code listing as the notification's contentIntent.

FIGURE 6.1 The notification pull-down in action!

This is the layout that will be inflated and placed into the notification bar. You can use only stock Android widgets for these (no custom views), and you'll want to keep it very simple. Mine consists of an icon and a text view. It's simple enough that you can probably imagine exactly what it looks like, but **Figure 6.1** shows what it looks like in action.

It's worth noting that you are not actually inflating the view yourself when creating a RemoteView. You're specifying a layout and then giving the system instructions on what to do to it when it is eventually inflated (this is the difference between a View and a RemoteView). You'll set this as the notification's contentView.

Next, you'll see me create an intent that is to be fired when the user presses on the notification row seen in Figure 6.1. This is a PendingIntent, which, again, is really an intent and an instruction about what to do with it when the time comes. In this case, I want to launch the activity with the Start and Stop buttons. You'll set the PendingIntent, as I did, to be the notification's contentIntent.

With the fully built notification in hand, you can now call startForeground and hand it the notification.

You've now met your half of the contract: You've told the user who you are and why you're running. The system now will allow you to run uninterrupted until such time as the user disables the service by pressing the activity's Stop button. It's time to start listening for when the content changes.

OBSERVING WHEN CONTENT CHANGES

Now that the service is running and in the foreground, I can show you what an empty ContentObserver looks like:

```
ContentObserver observer = new ContentObserver(null) {
    public void onChange(boolean self){
    }
};
```

Each time *any* photo on the phone changes, onChange will be called. It is your task, at that time, to determine what change actually took place. You should do this by querying the ContentProvider for images that were created after the lastUpdate Time. Here's what that looks like in my sample code:

```
Cursor cursor = null;
try {
    cursor = getContentResolver().query(
        MediaStore.Images.Media.EXTERNAL_CONTENT_URI, null,
        MediaStore.Images.Media.DATE_TAKEN + " > "+lastUpdateTime,
        null, null);
} finally {
    if(cursor!= null)
    cursor.close();
}
```

If this looks similar to a SQL query, it's meant to. I'm specifying the URI that I want information about (all images). The next parameter (to which I pass null) would be my chance to list the specific columns I want to receive. By passing null, I've asked for all of them. Next is the WHERE clause of the query, where I'm asking for every photo created after the lastUpdateTime. Since I don't have any more statements, I'll leave the next parameter null. Finally, the default sorting of results will suffice so I can pass null for the last parameter. Theoretically, the cursor should contain exactly one image. Here's how I process the cursor coming back from the ContentProvider:

```
lastUpdateTime = System.currentTimeMillis();
if(cursor.moveToFirst()){
    Intent i = new Intent(ACTION_PHOTO_TAKEN);
    int dataIDX = cursor.getColumnIndex(MediaStore.Images.Media.DATA);
    i.putExtra("path", cursor.getString(dataIDX));
    sendBroadcast(i);
}
```

TIP: Uploading photos: Normally, instead of calling send-Broadcast, I'd spin up another service (or an AsyncTask) to upload the photo to my favorite photo-sharing service. These services change so often that it's probably not worth spelling out exactly how to accomplish such a thing for Twitter, Flickr, Tumblr, or Imgur. If you want to implement your own, use the photo-downloading IntentService from Chapter 4 as a framework and go from there.

Now that I have the cursor, I can set the new lastUpdateTime. This will ensure that this current picture will not show up in subsequent observer-fired queries. Instead of starting an upload, I'm just sending an alert that a photo was taken and where you can find that new file. I then move the cursor to its initial position and make sure (by checking to see if it returns true) that there is actually a piece of data to find. Next, I'll get the column index for the data column. Last, I'll retrieve the path from the cursor and add it as an extra to my new intent. Last, I broadcast the existence of the photo for anyone who might be listening for it.

It's important to call cursor.close on every cursor you get back from a Content Provider. Otherwise, the system will throw errors at you for leaking memory.

BINDER SERVICE COMMUNICATION

On the very opposite side of the spectrum from intent-based communication is a service controlled through a binder interface. This allows cross-process communication with any other component that binds itself to your service. More than one process or component can bind with any service singleton, but they will, of course, all be accessing the same one.

Binding—and subsequently calling methods directly on the service—requires a few steps in order to handle the exchange cleanly and efficiently.

1. Create the interface with an AIDL file.

2. Create a service stub to return as the `IBinder` object.

3. Implement a `ServiceConnection` in order to make the connection with the service.

As you can see, this is not to be embarked upon unless you really need tight integration between your component and the service to which you'd like to bind.

In a later chapter, I'll show you the ins and outs of media playback and recording. To do this correctly, you're going to need the kind of integration that only a service with a bound interface can provide. So, by way of example, I'm going to build a background service with an `IBinder` suitable to play music in the background. For brevity, I'll avoid discussing every single method, but I'll cover a few basic functions and show you how to establish the connection.

CREATING AN AIDL

The AIDL (Android Interface Definition Language) file is your chance to define the interface through which your service can talk to the outside world. In my example, I created the `IMusicService.aidl` file in the `src/com/haseman/serviceExample/` directory. In it, you'll declare an interface:

```
package com.haseman.serviceExample;
interface IMusicService
{
    void pause();
        void play();
    void setDataSource(in long id);
    String getSongTitle();
}
```

More methods will eventually be needed for a fully functional music service, but for now this will do. When you next compile your project, Android will create an IMusicService.java file (you can find it in Eclipse under the gen package) containing all the Java code required to marshal the appropriate data across processes.

You might be wondering what that in prefix is doing in front of the parameter declaration of setDataSource. This is how you tell the service that, in this case, the service is the roach motel of method calls. The parameter goes in, but it doesn't come out (you won't be modifying or changing it within your service). This allows Android to marshal the variable across the processes once, but it means that it doesn't have to marshal it back out again, saving time and resources.

CREATING ANOTHER SERVICE

You're so good at creating services that I don't even need to walk you through doing it. I'm going to make myself a new service just as I did before. But this time, when you declare it, put it in a different process:

```
<service android:name="MusicService"
        android:process=":music_service"/>
```

The colon (:) in the process tells the system to prefix your current package name to it; otherwise, you can name the process anything you want. This way, the system can keep your music service running in the background while, at the same time, being able to shut down your larger application process, which is very handy on resource-constrained phones.

In the new service, I've declared all the same methods I had in the AIDL interface file. It currently looks like this:

```
public class MusicService extends Service{
    private void pause(){
    }
    private void play(){
    }
    public void setDataSource(long id){
    }
    public String getSongTitle(){
        return null;
    }
    @Override
    public IBinder onBind(Intent intent) {
        return null;
    }
}
```

CREATING THE BINDER AND AIDL STUB

Now that you have an interface and the methods in the service, it's time to connect the two. You'll need to do this using a stub. The stub keeps a weak reference to the service while also implementing your AIDL interface. It's also the object you'll pass back—instead of null—to the onBind call. You can declare it inside your service (although you don't actually have to). Here's what my stub looks like (complete with my new onBind call to return it back to the system):

```
private final IBinder mBinder = new MusicServiceStub(this);
@Override
public IBinder onBind(Intent intent) {
    return mBinder;
}
static class MusicServiceStub extends IMusicService.Stub {
        WeakReference<MusicService> mService;
        MusicServiceStub(MusicService service) {
            mService = new WeakReference<MusicService>(service);
        }
        public void pause(){
            mService.get().pause();
        }
        public void play(){
            mService.get().play();
        }
        public void setDataSource(long id){
            mService.get().setDataSource(id);
        }
        public String getSongTitle(){
            return mService.get().getSongTitle();
        }
}
```

You can see how it extends the IMusicService.Stub class and takes, in its constructor, a pointer to the outer service that it wraps in a weak reference. You need to do this because the system may keep a reference to the binder stub long after the service's onDestroy method has been called, and you'll want the garbage collector to be able clean up your service. For the curious, the weak reference allows the wrapped class to be deallocated by the garbage collector if the weak reference is the only remaining pointer to it. Quite handy in this case, assuming Android actually honors weak references.

You can also see how I'm returning this as the IBinder object when onBind is called. This MusicServiceStub will be the object that other components use to communicate with the service.

BINDING AND COMMUNICATING WITH THE SERVICE

You now have all the components you need to communicate, across a process, with your service. It's time to establish the connection.

I've added two more buttons to my service example activity to bind and unbind from my new skeleton music service. Here's what I've added to my OnClickListener to support them:

```
Intent bindServiceIntent =
    new Intent(getApplicationContext(), MusicService.class);
if(v.getId() == R.id.start_binder_service) {
    bindService(bindServiceIntent, this, Service.START_NOT_STICKY);
} else if(v.getId() == R.id.stop_binder_service) {
    unbindService(this);
}
```

You can see, in the highlighted code, that I'm binding with the service by giving it

- An intent specifying which service I'd like to connect to.

- A pointer to a ServiceConnection object (which I'll make my activity implement).

- A flag telling the system how I'd like the service started (in this case, not sticky—you can check the SDK documentation for more information about this one).

Now, my example code won't compile until I actually add an `implements Service Connection` to my activity's class declaration and the required methods that it entails. Here, in all their glory, are my activity's new required methods.

```
IMusicService mService;
@Override
public void onServiceConnected(ComponentName name, IBinder service) {
    mService = IMusicService.Stub.asInterface(service);
    try {
        mService.setDataSource(0);
    } catch (RemoteException re) { Log.e("MusicService", "",re}
}
@Override
public void onServiceDisconnected(ComponentName name) {
}
```

This code might look a little strange, but the `asInterface` call is converting from the `IBinder` object to the `IMusicService` (which I can then make direct calls on). However, each call to the remote service requires that you catch potential `RemoteExceptions` that come up.

That's really all there is to it. Once you've received the `onServiceConnected` call and completed the conversion, you can stash that `MusicService` object for whenever you need it.

But don't forget to unbind from it when your `onDestroy` method gets called.

Creating an AIDL and binding to a service in this way is actually one of the more complicated ways to communicate with a service. If you're not going to be building a long-running service in a separate process, this might not be the perfect setup for you. Consider checking the SDK documentation for the locally bound service or messenger patterns.

WRAPPING **UP**

In this chapter, you learned how to use a simple foreground service to notify you when a photograph is added to Android's `ContentProvider`. You learned how to start it, place it in the foreground with a notification, and then kill it off when the user no longer wanted it to run. Next, I went from the simple to the complex and showed you how to communicate directly with a service across process boundaries. You did this by creating an AIDL interface, implementing a stub, and then using a `ServiceConnection` and a `bindService` call to establish a connection with the service.

The first example was a simple service that does only one thing, while the second example you stormed through was one of the more complex mechanisms that Android can provide. If your arms are long enough (and you're not a *Tyrannosaurus rex*), give yourself a resounding pat on the back.

7

MANY **DEVICES,** ONE **APPLICATION**

Android devices have hundreds of different hardware configurations, from advanced TVs to very basic phones. Writing an application that runs perfectly across the whole spectrum can seem like a daunting task. Android, fortunately, provides many tools to handle the ecosystem on which it runs. In this chapter, I'll show you how to leverage Android's layout folder hierarchy system, configure your manifest to ensure that your application is available only to phones that can run it correctly, and handle older versions of the Android SDK. Android's diversity can be a challenge, but I'll show you how to use the available tools to make it a manageable one. This chapter covers the secrets of the res/ folder; weeding out devices with the manifest; and accommodating older phones with reflection.

UNCOVERING THE **SECRETS** OF THE **RES/** FOLDER

Earlier, I gave you a basic mapping of what goes where in the res/ folder. In this section, I'll show you its more advanced functions. As always, you can either code this yourself or follow along from the sample code posted at Peachpit.com/androiddevelopanddesign.

LAYOUT FOLDERS

The layout folders are the source of the first tool at your disposal, and it's one of the best. Android will, if configured correctly, pick layout files from a folder that matches the hardware configuration closest to the one it's running on. Using this tool, you can define multiple screen layouts for any number of different hardware configurations. Let's start with something simple: landscape mode.

Let's say you have a simple screen with two buttons. Let's take a look at the layout XML that produced the two buttons.

```
<RelativeLayout>
<!--Text view for question and relative layout params omitted-->
<Button
    android:padding="15dp"
    android:gravity="center"
    android:id="@+id/yes_button"
    android:layout_marginLeft="30dp"
    android:layout_marginRight="30dp"
    android:layout_width="fill_parent"
    android:layout_height="wrap_content"
    android:layout_above="@+id/no_button"
    android:text="@string/yes_button_text"
    />
<Button
    android:padding="15dp"
    android:gravity="center"
    android:id="@+id/no_button"
```

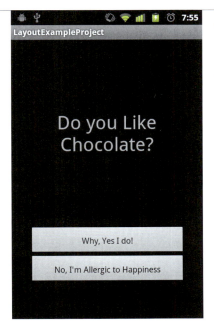

FIGURE 7.1 A simple screen with two buttons.

FIGURE 7.2 The buttons are far too large in landscape mode.

```
    android:layout_marginLeft="30dp"
    android:layout_marginRight="30dp"
    android:layout_marginBottom="60dp"
    android:layout_width="fill_parent"
    android:layout_height="wrap_content"
    android:text="@string/no_button_text"
    android:layout_alignParentBottom="true"
    />
```

What you see in this code listing shouldn't be anything new, given your experience with the RelativeLayout in previous chapters. I've declared two buttons, pinned the No button to the bottom, and aligned the Yes button above it. When shown in portrait mode, these buttons look simple but pretty good (**Figure 7.1**).

While this will only win me a design award if the judges are partially blind, it's a fairly good-looking, simple, and functional screen. But take a look at what happens when I switch it to landscape mode (**Figure 7.2**).

This is, for lack of a better term, a disaster. The buttons are far too wide in proportion to both their text and the "Do You Like Chocolate?" question above them. This is exactly the sort of problem that Android's layout folders make easy to solve.

In order to the fix this graphical mess, I need the buttons to be side by side in landscape mode while still being stacked in portrait mode. There are two approaches to fixing this problem: a slightly heavy-handed method involving setting up a second screen layout for landscape, or using a scalpel to excise and fix only the parts that are broken. Both solutions have their place.

USING DIFFERENT FOLDERS

Android allows you to specify different layout folders for various hardware screen configurations. This example solves the problem by adding a layout-land folder to your project.

Now we come to the magic part.

1. Create a new folder named `layout-land` for the landscape configuration, and place it in *project*/res/.

2. Into this folder, place landscape-specific layout files that Android will use *automatically* when the device is in landscape mode.

USING <INCLUDE> FOR SMALL CHANGES

The `<include>` tag is a fantastic way to pull out small portions of your screen that you'd like to tweak and lay out separately. This is the scalpel method. You cut out only the portions you want to render differently, you split them into folder-separated layouts, and you're finished. Which, in this case, is a perfect way to excise the buttons and have them render differently depending on the screen orientation. Here's how to do exactly that.

1. Create a new `button_layout.xml` file in res/layout-land/.

   This is the file into which we'll put the landscape-specific layout.

2. Add a `LinearLayout` and two `Buttons` in the new `button_layout.xml` file, and place them next to each other in the new horizontal linear layout. Here's the final contents of my /layout-land/button_layout.xml.

```xml
<?xml version="1.0" encoding="utf-8"?>
<LinearLayout
    xmlns:android="http://schemas.android.com/apk/res/android"
    android:orientation="horizontal"
    android:layout_width="match_parent"
    android:layout_height="wrap_content"
    android:layout_marginBottom="60dp"
    android:layout_alignParentBottom="true"
    >
    <Button
        android:padding="15dp"
        android:gravity="center"
        android:id="@+id/yes_button"
        android:layout_marginLeft="20dp"
        android:layout_marginRight="5dp"
        android:layout_width="fill_parent"
        android:layout_height="wrap_content"
        android:text="@string/yes_button_text"
        android:layout_weight="50"
        />
    <Button
        android:padding="15dp"
        android:gravity="center"
        android:id="@+id/no_button"
        android:layout_marginLeft="5dp"
        android:layout_marginRight="20dp"
        android:layout_width="fill_parent"
        android:layout_height="wrap_content"
```

```
        android:text="@string/no_button_text"

        android:layout_weight="50"

        />

</LinearLayout>
```

As you can see, I've created a horizontal layout with two buttons to be used in landscape mode.

Don't forget about the portrait layout. If we're going to include a layout, it's got to exist for both the landscape configuration and the default configuration.

3. Create a new button_layout.xml file in /res/layout/ (or you could add it as /res/layout-port/button_layout.xml). I've just copied the original buttons' code and pasted it into a new RelativeLayout:

```
<?xml version="1.0" encoding="utf-8"?>

<RelativeLayout

    xmlns:android="http://schemas.android.com/apk/res/android"

    android:layout_marginBottom="60dp"

    android:layout_width="fill_parent"

    android:layout_height="100dp"

    android:layout_alignParentBottom="true"

    >

    <Button

        android:padding="15dp"

        android:gravity="center"

        android:id="@+id/yes_button"

        android:layout_marginLeft="30dp"

        android:layout_marginRight="30dp"

        android:layout_width="fill_parent"

        android:layout_height="wrap_content"
```

```
        android:layout_above="@+id/no_button"
        android:text="@string/yes_button_text"
        />
    <Button
        android:padding="15dp"
        android:gravity="center"
        android:id="@+id/no_button"
        android:layout_marginLeft="30dp"
        android:layout_marginRight="30dp"
        android:layout_width="fill_parent"
        android:layout_height="wrap_content"
        android:text="@string/no_button_text"
        android:layout_alignParentBottom="true"
    />
</RelativeLayout>
```

At this point, you've created two layouts: one for portrait and one for landscape.

4. You can now modify your original XML with an `include`, like so:

```
<RelativeLayout>
<!--Text view and relative layout params omitted-->
<include layout="@layout/button_layout"
        android:id="@+id/button_holder"
    />
</RelativeLayout>
```

With the `<include>` tag in place (instead of a single button definition), Android will grab the `button_layout.xml` file that corresponds to the screen configuration. If it can't find one, it will default back to what's in `/res/layout`.

FIGURE 7.3 No awards for design, but much better.

Now, with this new code, the landscape mode looks much better (**Figure 7.3**).

Are there things that could be improved? Sure! Now, however, you know how to specify that parts of your user interface should change as the screen's hardware configuration changes.

MERGING

You don't have to wrap your excised views in a new ViewGroup (RelativeLayout in the previous example) for them to be included (as I did here). If you don't want to add another layout to the mix but would like to bring in a series of views from other XML files, simply wrap them in a <merge> tag.

```
<merge xmlns:android="http://schemas.android.com/apk/res/android">
<!-- views go here -->
</merge>
```

This will allow you to include views without adding another layout to your view hierarchy.

WHAT CAN YOU DO BEYOND LANDSCAPE?

Lots. You can add suffixes to layout folders to account for just about everything. Here are a few I use on a regular basis.

- `layout-small, layout-normal, layout-large, layout-xlarge`

  The size modifier accounts for the physical size of the screen. Devices that would use the small layout folder are typically very old, or very strange pieces of hardware, at least until Android powered watches become popular. Most modern phones fit the `layout-normal` category, while many tablets are considered `xlarge`. Google keeps a great breakdown of all the various screen configurations at http://developer.android.com/resources/dashboard/screens.html.

- `layout-ldpi, layout-mdpi, layout-hdpi, layout-xhdpi`

  The dpi, or dots per inch, of the device is a measurement of screen *density*. Screens with high densities (240 dpi) would pull from the layout folder `layout-hdpi`.

- `layout-large-hdpi-land`

  You can also mix and match the suffixes. This suffix would be used for phones that have large screens and high resolution and that are in landscape mode. Get creative, but remember that just because you can get very specific about screen configurations, it doesn't mean you should.

THE FULL SCREEN DEFINE

Just as you can place separate layout files to be referenced in `<include>` for different hardware configurations, so can you define a completely different screen in the `layout-land` folder for the system to use in landscape mode. This might seem like the best course of action at first, but it is less than ideal for several reasons.

- It involves a lot of typing.

  Instead of defining two small parts that change based on the screen configuration, you have to make and test more than one entire screen layout.

- Making changes can be painful.

  With many hardware configurations comes a plethora of different screens. Were you to fully lay out a screen for every configuration, you'd have a nightmare on your hands when your designer wants to remove or add a button. You would have to add it separately to each XML file for every single screen configuration.

Those two things aside, sometimes you really do need a completely separate layout for a different hardware or screen configuration. Try to modify small parts when you can, but don't be afraid to crack your knuckles and make a totally new screen layout when it's necessary.

To make a new layout of the "chocolate" example, you can simply make a second `two_buttons.xml` file in `/res/layout-land` and configure the screen in any way you like. Then the call to `setContentView` in the `onCreate` method of your activity will, like `include`, find the right resource for the right screen configuration.

HOW CAN THIS POSSIBLY WORK?

That's a great question that I'm glad you asked only at the end of the section. Because it separates layout files from activities, Android can have any number of different layouts for the myriad of possible screen configurations. You simply specify the layout name, and Android goes off in search of the correct XML file to show the user. To keep this process running smoothly, keep the following things in mind:

- The layouts *must* share the same name.

  Android can only find the layout XML by name. As long as the layout files have the exact same filename, it will locate the version in your landscape (or any other) folder.

- Make sure that the IDs for your individual views are consistent.

  Remember that your activity calls `findViewById` in order to manipulate and interact with onscreen objects. The activity shouldn't care where a view is to register a click listener, set an image, or pull data from an `EditText`.

- Try not to move views around in your activity's Java code.

  Your activity shouldn't try to change the position of things onscreen. While in portrait mode, the button might be at point (330, 120); it will be somewhere totally different in landscape mode. In this situation, adding more screen layouts will require also adding the corresponding movement code to your activity, and this can become time consuming.

BE CAREFUL

Debugging layout issues across many linked layout files can be exhausting (I've done it), so keep your layouts as stretchy and dynamic as you possibly can. If your designs are done well, they should be able to automatically handle many screen resolutions with good use of linear and relative layouts. Fall back on includes and multiple layout folders only when dynamic layouts can't do the job. There will be times, however, when one layout doesn't do all screens justice. When this happens, make your breakouts as small and efficient as possible. Don't hesitate to use this amazing layout tool, but be careful not to use it too much.

LIMITING **ACCESS** TO YOUR **APP** TO **DEVICES** THAT **WORK**

Your Android application may, in a lot of cases, require some very specific hardware in order to work correctly. I imagine that users who, for example, download a camera app to a device that doesn't have a camera will have a very poor experience.

THE <USES> TAG

Android gives you an avenue to tell the marketplace which devices it should allow to download and purchase your application. This is done with the <uses> tag in your AndroidManifest.xml file.

If, for example, your app requires the device to have a camera, you should add the following line to your manifest:

```
<uses-feature android:name="android.hardware.camera"
  android:required="true"/>
```

This line tells Android that the application should not be installed on a device without a camera, because it's required for correct operation. You can, on the flip side, declare that your app use a particular piece of hardware, but degrade appropriately if it's not there. An image-editing app might want the camera, but if the camera's not there it may still function by modifying images saved from the web in the device's built-in gallery. You tell the system this by declaring the hardware as used but setting the requirement to false:

```
<uses-feature android:name="android.hardware.camera"
  android:required="false"/>
```

There are a host of hardware features you can set. It's probably best to check the documentation for the full list (http://developer.android.com/guide/topics/manifest/uses-feature-element.html).

SDK VERSION NUMBER

You can also declare which versions of the SDK your application supports. You do this by declaring <uses-sdk> in your manifest. In fact, if you created your project using Eclipse or the Android command-line tools, you already have a basic declaration:

```
<uses-sdk android:minSdkVersion="10" />
```

You can add minimum and maximum supported SDKs if there are classes or objects you rely on that aren't available on older devices. You can, however, block out older and newer versions of the SDK with a declaration that looks like this:

```
<uses-sdk
    android:maxSdkVersion="10"
    android:minSdkVersion="6" />
```

This will tell the Android Market to list the associated application for devices that are SDK 6: Android 2.0.1 update 1 and above. It will also block devices greater than Gingerbread from running your software. Further, if you try to load the app through a web link, the downloader will block the install on the grounds that the application isn't supported.

It's worth mentioning that this sort of heavy-handed blocking should really be a last-ditch effort. If you can make your application work well with both the latest and oldest devices, you should. With this declaration, you can limit who is allowed to install your app.

HANDLING CODE IN OLDER ANDROID VERSIONS

I can't tell you how many times I've found the *perfect* Android SDK class to solve some annoying problem, only to find out that its use is limited to the latest version of the SDK. There is one trick you can use when faced with code that will compile only on later versions of Android: reflection.

While reflection is in no way unique to Android (it's built into Java), it is something you can use to protect older phones from newfangled classes and methods.

SHAREDPREFERENCES AND APPLY

Long ago, in a galaxy that's actually quite close, Google figured out that writing to disk on the main thread is a bad thing for performance. During this discovery, they found that the SharedPreferences (something that's typically used to save user settings and preferences) do actually write to disk when you save them through their commit method. You'll see what I'm talking about in the following method, which saves a username to the preferences:

```
public void setUsername(String username){
    SharedPreferences prefs =
        PreferenceManager.getDefaultSharedPreferences(this);
    Editor ed = prefs.edit();
        ed.putString("username", username);
    ed.commit();
}
```

This works just fine, but as it turns out, commit writes to the disk, and calling this on the main thread is a no-no (for reasons we've discussed at length). In SDK version 9, however, Google introduced the apply method to the SharedPreferences Editor class. Again, this is great, but there's a catch: Any device that tries to use a class containing the apply method will throw a validation exception and crash. So how, you might be wondering, do I use apply on Android SDK 9 (2.3.3) and higher without breaking any 2.2 (or earlier) devices?

REFLECTING YOUR TROUBLES AWAY

The solution for this problem, and indeed all problems with later declared SDK methods, is to access them using reflection. Reflection allows you to use Java methods without explicitly defining or including them in your code. It's perfect for handling these kinds of situations.

Ideally, I'd like to call apply if it's available (SDK 9 and higher) but fall back to commit if apply is going to cause problems. Here's the new version of setUsername to do exactly that:

```
public void setUsername(String username){
    SharedPreferences prefs =
        PreferenceManager.getDefaultSharedPreferences(this);
    Editor ed = prefs.edit();
    ed.putString("username", username);
    try{
        Method applyMethod =
            Editor.class.getDeclaredMethod("apply",
                new Class[]{});
        if(applyMethod != null)
            applyMethod.invoke(ed, new Object[]{});
        else
            ed.commit();
    }catch(Exception error){
        ed.commit();
    }
}
```

While this method starts the same as the previous one—getting the Editor and using it to save the string—it diverges when it comes time to save that username.

Reflection can throw several different errors (the major one to look out for is MethodNotFoundException), so the reflection calls will need to be wrapped in a try catch block. I'm first requesting the apply method from the Editor class. If I get it (and it isn't null, it doesn't throw an exception, and the lunar phase is exactly right), I'll then be able to invoke it (again through the reflection call) and we're done. If it isn't found as part of the SharedPreferences Editor class, I'll fall back on calling commit. Reflection allows me to define and use methods that may not be compiled into earlier versions of the SDK.

ALWAYS KEEP AN EYE ON API LEVELS

In the Android documentation, each class and method has a small gray label reading "Since: API Level #" on the right-hand side. If that number is higher than the system you'd like to support, you may need to re-evaluate using that class or method.

Reflection allows you to have the best of both worlds. You can use these latest methods on newer devices that support them, while gracefully degrading on devices that don't.

Keep in mind, however, that reflection is slow and potentially error prone, so use it sparingly and with care. If you're going to be frequently using a class or method that has two different implementations (Contacts, for example), consider using conditional class loading instead. That is, write two Adapter classes for each version of the class (one for the old, one for the new), and use whichever one is supported. You can always find out which SDK your device is running by checking android.os.Build.Version.SDK.

WRAPPING **UP**

In this chapter, you learned how to handle diversity in screen resolution, density, and configuration. You did this through advanced use of the layout folders, the `<include>` tag, and Android's XML layout system. Then you learned how to tell Android which device features you require by putting declarations in the manifest. Last, you learned about using reflection to take advantage of advanced methods when they're available and to avoid them when they're not.

Given all these tools, you should be ready to bring your killer mobile application into play on the tremendous number of devices—from refrigerators to phones to televisions—available to you on the Android platform.

In any case, monotony is boring. Different devices allow for innovation, greater user choice, and funny-looking screen protectors. Now that you're equipped to handle it, you'll be scaling resources and rocking the landscape mode with ease.

8

MOVIES AND MUSIC

Support for media, both audio and visual, will hopefully be an essential part of your next immersive Android application. Both industries are ripe for reinvention, and the next media format revolution almost certainly will involve mobile devices. To this end, I'll get you started with the basics for Android's video and music libraries in this chapter. I'll also point out a few things you'll need to be aware of as you build a background media playback service: movies, music playback, background service, and what to watch out for.

MOVIES

Movie playback on an Android device boils down to the `VideoView` class. In this section, I'll use a simple example application that will play through every video saved on a phone's SD card. Here is the general process:

- I'll use the `ContentProvider` (something you'll remember from our brief discussion in Chapter 6 when we uploaded the most recent photo) to request every video saved to the user's external card.

- After loading a `Cursor` (Android's query result data object) with all the device's videos, I'll need a method to play the next one.

- I'll set up an activity as a listener so that when video playback is complete, I can call my `playNextVideo` method and move on to the next video in the cursor.

- Last, I'll clean up after my cursor when the user leaves the playback screen.

Before I can do any of these things, however, I need to place a `VideoView` on my main layout to work with.

ADDING A VIDEOVIEW

Placing a `VideoView` onscreen is as simple as adding it to your XML layout. Here's what my `main.xml` file now looks like:

```
<?xml version="1.0" encoding="utf-8"?>

<LinearLayout xmlns:android="http://schemas.android.com/
    apk/res/android"

    android:orientation="vertical"

    android:layout_width="match_parent"

    android:layout_height="match_parent"

    >

<VideoView

    android:layout_width="match_parent"

    android:layout_height="match_parent"

    android:id="@+id/my_video_view"

    />

</LinearLayout>
```

Once the video view is in the screen's layout, you can retrieve it, as you would any other view, with findViewById. I'm going to need access to the video view later when it's time to switch videos. Instead of retrieving the view with findViewById each time, I'll add a private data member to my Activity class. Next, I'll need to configure the video player.

SETTING UP FOR THE VIDEOVIEW

In the following code listing, I'm doing many normal onCreate sorts of things.

```
VideoView videoView = null;
@Override
public void onCreate(Bundle savedInstanceState) {
    super.onCreate(savedInstanceState);
    setContentView(R.layout.main);
    videoView = (VideoView)findViewById(R.id.my_video_view);
        videoView.setOnCompletionListener(this);
}
```

Here I'm setting the content view, retrieving and caching the video view with findViewById, and setting my activity as the video view's onCompletionListener.

In order for the activity to pass itself into the VideoView as the onCompletion Listener, I have to extend OnCompletionListener and implement my own onCompletion method. Here is what I've added to my activity:

```
public class MediaExampleActivity extends Activity
        implements OnCompletionListener{
    @Override
    public void onCompletion(MediaPlayer mp) {
    }
    //Rest of Activity code omitted
}
```

I now have a configured, yet very simplistic, video player. You'll most likely want to have visual onscreen controls. Android's VideoView allows you to implement and set up a MediaController for the VideoView class. If you're looking to go further into video playback after this chapter, this would be an excellent place to start.

GETTING MEDIA TO PLAY

Now that my video view is ready to roll, I can start hunting for things for it to actually play. For this simple example, I'm going to play every video on the device one after another until they're all finished. To achieve this, I'll use Android's media ContentProvider (accessed with a call to getContentResolver). I'll show you the code and then dig into some specifics. Here's what onCreate looks like with the new code to fetch a cursor with all the media objects:

```
Cursor mediaCursor = null;
VideoView videoView = null;
int dataIdx = 0;
@Override
public void onCreate(Bundle savedInstanceState) {
    super.onCreate(savedInstanceState);
    setContentView(R.layout.main);
    videoView = (VideoView)findViewById(R.id.my_video_view);
    videoView.setOnCompletionListener(this);
    String projection[] = new String[] {Video.Media.DATA};
    mediaCursor =
        getContentResolver().query(
            Video.Media.EXTERNAL_CONTENT_URI,
            projection, null, null, null);
    if(mediaCursor != null && mediaCursor.getCount() > 0){
        dataIdx = mediaCursor.getColumnIndex(Video.Media.DATA);
        playNextVideo();
    }
}
```

As you can see, I'm still fetching and caching the video view, but now I'm issuing a query to Android's ContentProvider for the DATA column of all media rows that are videos. Specifically, you can see this in action in the highlighted code. That query is fairly simple in that I want all videos on the external drive (SD card), and I only care about the data column for all those rows. This column for any particular row should always contain the path to the actual media content on disk. It's this path that I'll eventually hand off to the VideoView for playback.

Note that it is possible to pass URIs to the video view. The video playback mechanism will find the path to the object for you. I would, however, like to show you the harder way so that you'll be more informed. And if you later need to upload or manipulate a file directly, you'll know how to acquire it.

The Cursor object (a class Android uses to wrap database query responses) can be null if the external media card is removed (or mounted into USB storage mode), so I'll need to check for a null cursor or one with no results before moving on. Typically in this case, I'd display a message to the user about their SD card being unavailable, but I'll leave that task up to your imagination.

Last, I'll get and cache the column index for the data row. This will make it easier for my playNextVideo method to interact with the cursor's results.

LOADING AND PLAYING MEDIA

At this point, you have a video view, a cursor full of media to play, and a listener configured to tell you when media playback is finished. Let's put the final piece into the game, the code in playNextVideo:

```
private void playNextVideo(){
        mediaCursor.moveToNext();
        if(mediaCursor.isAfterLast()){
            Toast.makeText(getApplicationContext(),
            "End of Line.", Toast.LENGTH_SHORT).show();
        }
        else{
            String path = mediaCursor.getString(dataIdx);
            Toast.makeText(getApplicationContext(),
            "Playing: "+path, Toast.LENGTH_SHORT).show();
            videoView.setVideoPath(path);
            videoView.start();
        }
    }
```

My first task is to move the cursor to the next piece of media and make sure we haven't run out of stuff to play. When I know I've got a valid row from the cursor, I can tell the video view what it should render next. Video views can accept both a path defined as a string as well as the URI for a piece of media declared in the content provider. As I mentioned earlier, the data column of the cursor contains the file path to the media itself. I'll pull this out of the Cursor, hand it off to the video view, and then start playback.

TIP: You're not limited to just file paths—you can hand the video view a URL, and it will query and play the media found there.

Recall that earlier I registered my activity as the OnCompletionListener for the video view so that when a video is finished it will notify me via the OnCompletion call. In that method, I just need to call back into my playNextVideo code and we're playing!

```
@Override
public void onCompletion(MediaPlayer mp) {
    playNextVideo();
}
```

At this point, the pieces are in place, videos play, and you're almost done!

CLEANUP

You've seen me do this at least once before, but it's always important to close any cursors you request from the content provider. In past cases, I've requested data with a query, pulled out the relevant information, and immediately closed the cursor. In this case, however, I need to keep the cursor around for when the video change has to occur. This does not get me off the hook; I still need to close it down, so I'll need to add that code to my activity's onDestroy method:

```
@Override
public void onDestroy(){
    if(mediaCursor!=null){
        mediaCursor.close();
    }
}
```

THE REST, AS THEY SAY, IS UP TO YOU

I've shown you the very basics of loading and playing video content. Now it's time for you to explore it on your own. Think about loading a video from a remote location (hint: encoding a URL as a URI) or building a progress bar (hint: getCurrentProgress calls on the VideoView).

Because errors are to media playback as swearing is to sailors, registering for an onErrorListener is never a bad idea. Android will, if you pass it a class that implements the OnErrorListener interface, tell you if it has hiccups playing your media files. As always, check the documentation for more information on playback.

MUSIC

Music playback, in general, revolves around the `MediaPlayer` class. This is in a sense very similar to what you've just done with the video view (except you don't need a `View` object to render into).

Media players, if used to play music, should end up in their own services, with one notable exception: games and application sound effects. Building a sound effect example will make for a very simple way to get into the basics of audio playback.

MEDIAPLAYER AND STATE

You do not simply walk into Mordor. Similarly, you do not simply run about playing things willy-nilly. It requires care, attention to detail, and an understanding of the media player's states. Here they are, in the order you're most likely to encounter them:

- Idle. In this state, the `MediaPlayer` doesn't know anything and, consequently, cannot actually do anything. To move on to the initialized state, you'll need to tell it which file it's going to play. This is done through the `setDataSource` method.

- Initialized. At this point, the media player knows what you'd like it to play, but it hasn't acquired the data to do so. This is particularly important to understand when dealing with playing remote audio from a URL. Calling `prepare` or `prepareAsync` will move it into the prepared state. It will also load enough data from either the file system or the Internet to be ready for playback.

- Prepared. After calling `prepare` or `prepareAsync` (and getting a callback), your media player is ready to rock! At this point, you can call `seek` (to move the playhead) or `start` (to begin playback).

- Playing. Audio is pumping, people are dancing (OK, maybe not), and life is good. In this state, you can call `pause` to halt the audio or `seek` to move the play position. You end the party by calling `stop`, which will move the media player back to the initialized state.

Just because you've run out of media to play doesn't mean your player drops into the idle state. It will keep the current file loaded if you want to call `start` (which will restart the audio from the beginning) or `seek` (to move the playhead to a particular place). Only when you call `stop` or `reset` does the `MediaPlayer` clear its buffers and return to the initialized state, ready for you to call `prepare` again.

PLAYING A SOUND

At its most straightforward, media playback is actually quite easy. Android gives you helper methods to shepherd your media player from the idle state to the prepared state if you can specify a file or resource id right away. In this example case, you can record your own WAV file or use the beeeep file that I included in the example project. I've added the file to the newly created /res/raw/ folder so the application can load it directly.

Further, I've added a button (which you should be a pro at by now) that, when pressed, will play the recorded audio. Once the button is defined (id beep_button) in the main.xml layout file and the audio beeeep.wav file is placed in the raw/ folder, the following code should work like a charm:

```
MediaPlayer mBeeper;
@Override
    public void onCreate(Bundle savedInstanceState) {
        super.onCreate(savedInstanceState);
        setContentView(R.layout.main);
        Button beep = (Button)findViewById(R.id.beep_button);
        beep.setOnClickListener(this);
        mBeeper =
        MediaPlayer.create(getApplicationContext(), R.raw.beeeep);
    }
```

As you can see, I'm retrieving the beep_button from the main.xml layout (which I told the activity would be my screen's layout) and setting my activity as the click listener for the button. Last, I use the media player's create helper method to initialize and prepare the media player with the beeeep.wav file from the raw/ directory.

PLAYING A SOUND EFFECT

Remember that loading media, even from the res/ folder, can take some time. With this in mind, I've added the media player as a private data member to my Activity class. This means I can load it once in my onCreate method and then use it every time the user presses the button. Speaking of button pressing, here's the code to play the sound effect when the button is pressed:

```
@Override
public void onClick(View v) {
    mBeeper.start();
}
```

CLEANUP

In order to be a good citizen, there's one more step you need to remember to take: releasing your resources! That's right, when your activity closes down, you need to tell the media player that you're finished with it, like so:

```
@Override
public void onDestroy(){
    if(mBeeper != null){
        mBeeper.stop();
        mBeeper.release();
        mBeeper = null;
    }
}
```

Checking for null before performing the cleanup is a good precaution. If, for whatever reason, there isn't enough memory to load the resource or it fails for another reason, you won't have any null pointer exceptions on your hands.

IT REALLY IS THAT SIMPLE

There's nothing complex about simple sound effect playback. Once you have a media player in the prepared state, you can call start on it as many times as you like to produce the desired effect. Just remember to clean it up once you're finished. Your users will thank you later. Now let's move on to something a little more tricky.

LONGER-RUNNING
MUSIC PLAYBACK

You didn't think I'd let you off that easy, did you? Remember two chapters ago when I showed you how to build a service in a separate process by using an AIDL file? I told you you'd need it for longer-running music playback. Here's a quick recap of that process:

1. Create a service, define a few methods to control music playback, and declare the service in your manifest.

2. Create an Android Interface Definition Language (AIDL) file to define how the service will talk to any of the activities.

3. Bind an activity to the service, and, when the callback is hit, save the binder in order to call the service's methods.

If most, or any, of those steps don't make sense, take a gander back at Chapter 6.
In this section, I'll show you how to turn the empty service into one that actually plays music in the background. The example music service will have methods to pause, play, set a data source, and ask it what the title of the current song is. To show you this service in practice, I'll have my activity play the most recently added song on my new background music service.

BINDING TO THE MUSIC SERVICE

There is a little overlap here with Chapter 6, but it's worth covering how this works again before I dive into the music service itself. I've added the following code to the onCreate method of our handy MusicExampleActivity.

```
public void onCreate(Bundle savedInstanceState) {

    //Button code omitted

    Intent serviceIntent =

    new Intent(getApplicationContext(), MusicService.class);

        startService(serviceIntent);

        bindService(serviceIntent, this, 0);

}
```

You'll notice that I'm actually starting the service before I attempt to bind to it. Although you can ask the bind service call to start the service for you, this is not a good idea when building a music service. That's because when you unbind from the service, which you must do whenever your activity is destroyed, it will shut the service down. This, as you might imagine, would be bad if you'd like music to continue playing in the background after your activity has closed.

FINDING THE MOST RECENT TRACK

I've added a button to my screen that, when pressed, will query Android's content provider for the most recent track. Assuming it has both a track to play and a valid service, I can start playing music. Here's the code that runs when the Play button is pressed:

```
public void onClick(View v) {
    CursorLoader cursorLoader = new
        CursorLoader(getApplicationContext(),
        MediaStore.Audio.Media.EXTERNAL_CONTENT_URI, null, null,
        null, MediaStore.Audio.Media.DATE_ADDED + " Desc Limit 1");
    cursorLoader.registerListener(0, this);
    cursorLoader.startLoading();
}
```

In this code, I'm using a cursor loader to fetch my rather bizarre query. I'm asking the content provider for all possible audio tracks, but I'm sorting the results in descending order of their addition date (that is, when they were added to the phone) and limiting it to one result. This will, when the loader finishes, return a cursor with one record (the most recent song added to the library).

Android, in version 3.0, added the Loader class to its arsenal of helpers. A loader is essentially a simplified version of the AsyncTask class. It processes or acquires a piece of data off the main thread and then calls your listener on the main thread when the data is ready. In this chapter, I'm giving it a query string that, if the user has a lot of media, could take a very long time. This is an excellent time to deploy one of Android's loader subclasses: the CursorLoader. You can user this library on versions of Android older than 3.0 by including the Android compatibility library in your project. To add it, right-click your project and select Android Tools > Add Compatibility Library.

When the cursor with my data is ready, my activity's onLoadComplete will be called, at which point I can tell my music service what to play:

```java
@Override
public void onLoadComplete(Loader<Cursor> loader, Cursor cursor) {
    if(!cursor.moveToFirst()){
        Toast.makeText(getApplicationContext(), "No Music to Play",
        → Toast.LENGTH_LONG).show();

        return;
    }
    int idIDX = cursor.getColumnIndex(MediaStore.Audio.Media._ID);
    long id = cursor.getLong(idIDX);
    if(mService == null){
        Toast.makeText(getApplicationContext(),
            "No Service to play Music!",
            Toast.LENGTH_LONG).show();
        return;
    }
    try{
        mService.setDataSource(id);
        mService.play();
```

```
        Button play = (Button)findViewById(R.id.most_recent_song);
        play.setText("Stop "+mService.getSongTitle());
    }catch(Exception E){
        Log.e("MusicPlayerActivity", "setData failed",E);
    }
    cursor.close();
}
```

When the loader hits my callback, I'll first need to check if it actually found any data. By checking if(!cursor.moveToFirst()){, I'm moving to the first and only record in the cursor, but I'm also making sure there actually is a record for me to look at. (If the cursor is empty, moveToFirst will return false.)

Next, I'll get the column index of the _ID column and call getLong on the cursor to acquire the media's unique ID. It is with this ID that I'll tell the music service what it should play.

I'll also need to make sure that my service bind in the onCreate method was successful. Once I know that the service is valid, I can tell it what entry I want it to play with setDataSource and then tell it to start playback with play.

PLAYING THE AUDIO IN THE SERVICE

Now that you can see how the ID is acquired, I'll switch over to the music service and show you how the handoff occurs over there. Here's what setDataSource looks like from the service's perspective (which we defined the skeleton for earlier):

```
Cursor mCursor;
MediaPlayer mPlayer = null;
public void setDataSource(long id){
    if(mCursor != null){
        mCursor.close();
    }
    mCursor =
```

```
            getContentResolver().query(
            MediaStore.Audio.Media.EXTERNAL_CONTENT_URI, null,
            MediaStore.Audio.Media._ID + " = "+ id, null, null);
        if(mCursor == null)
            return;
        if(!mCursor.moveToFirst()){
            mCursor.close();
            mCursor = null;
            return;
        }
        int pathIDX = mCursor.getColumnIndex(MediaStore.Audio.Media.DATA);
        String path = mCursor.getString(pathIDX);
        try{
            mPlayer.reset();
            mPlayer.setDataSource(path);
            mPlayer.prepare();
        }catch(IOException io){
            Log.e("MediaService", "Unable to set data source",io);
        }
    }
```

While this code is a little bit long, most of it should look similar to tasks you've already done.

1. I'm querying the content provider for the id passed into the method.

2. I'm making sure that the music is actually there first by checking if the cursor came back null (which can happen if the SD card has been removed). I'm also checking that there's a valid row in the cursor.

It's worth noting, again, that I've taken the harder of two routes here. Instead of querying the content provider for the exact media path, I could build a URI for the media in question and hand it off instead. I've taken what may be a slightly more complex route to playback only so that when you'd like to get to the file itself, you'll know how.

3. When I'm sure the cursor is valid and contains the data for a song to play, I can reset the player (in case it was already playing something else), set the data source for it, and tell the media player to prepare. Once these methods are done, the media player is ready to start playback.

With that, your service is ready to go when the activity calls play.

PLAY TIME

Now that the service has a data source and is prepared, the activity can call play, which will trigger the following code to run:

```
private void play(){
    if(mPlayer != null){
        mPlayer.start();
        setForegroundState(true);
    }
}
```

You'll need to start media playback and make sure the service switches to running in the foreground. setForegroundState is a method I defined back in Chapter 6 that places an icon in the notification screen. If you need a refresher on how to put services into foreground mode, review Chapter 6 or look at the sample code for this chapter.

ALL GOOD THINGS MUST END . . . HOPEFULLY

At some point, the music has to stop—either because it's run out of songs to play or because the user has killed it off. My sample code includes a stop method, but because it looks almost exactly like the play method I listed in the last section, it doesn't bear spelling out here. However, because I wanted the service to last beyond the run of my activity, I'll need to have the service close itself down. You can find the appropriate time to shut down the service by registering it as an onCompletion Listener with the media player. The line of code looks like this:

```
mPlayer.setOnCompletionListener(this);
```

You can call it at any point after the player is created. Of course, your service will need to implement OnCompletionListener and have the correct onCompletion method.

```
@Override
public void onCompletion(MediaPlayer mp) {
    stopSelf();
}
```

This means that once the media is finished, the service will call stop on itself, which, because of the lifecycle of the service, will trigger Android to call the service's onDestroy method—the perfect place to clean up. Once the cleanup is finished, the service will be deallocated and cease running.

CLEANUP

Cleanup is essential when dealing with cursors and media players. If you don't handle this section correctly, a lot of the device's memory can get lost in the shuffle. Here's the onDestroy method where I clean up both the cursor and the media player:

```
@Override
public void onDestroy(){
    super.onDestroy();
    if(mCursor != null)
```

```
        mCursor.close();
    if(mPlayer != null) {
        mPlayer.stop();
        mPlayer.release();
    }
}
```

I must be careful, because an incorrect data source ID or bad media file could leave either of these pointers `null`, which would crash the service quite handily when I try to shut them down.

INTERRUPTIONS

When you're writing music software for Android devices, it's vitally important that you remember that the hardware on which your software is running is, in fact, a *phone*. This means you'll need to watch out for several things.

- Audio focus. You'll need to use the `AudioManager` class (introduced in Android 2.2) to register an audio focus listener, because other applications may want to play alerts, navigational directions, or their own horrible music. This is vital to making an Android music playback application play nice with the rest of the system.

- Controls built into headphones. You'll want your service to register to receive headset button intents through your manifest (or at runtime when your service is started). At the very least, set your service up to pause when the headset control is clicked.

- Phone calls. By watching the phone's call state either through the `Telephony Manager` or with the audio focus tools, you *absolutely* must watch for incoming phone calls. You must stop all audio when the phone rings. Nothing will enrage your users (and hurt your ratings) more than not accommodating phone calls.

- Missing SD card. You'll want to make sure your app handles a missing or removed SD card correctly. Users can mount their external cards as removable drives with the USB cable at any point. Android will alert you if you listen for the `ACTION_MEDIA_REMOVED` intent.

This might seem like a lot of things to look out for (and it is), but never fear, the developers at Google have released an open source media player (which they ship with the Android source code) that can be a great guide for dealing with this stuff. As always, the documentation will have a lot on the subject as well.

WRAPPING UP

In this chapter, I showed you how to

- Play a simple video

- Play a sound effect when a button is pressed

- Take a previously created service interface and create a functional media player from it

You should now be comfortable with the essentials for media playback. If you're looking to go further with videos (which I hope you are), you'll want to look into using a controller to modify the state of the video view.

Your next step to expand the media playback service is to think about how you'd pass arrays of IDs (playlists) and how you'd deal with updating those playlists on the fly (as users change them).

Android can be a very powerful media platform if you're careful and treat it with care. Go forth and make a crop of better music players—if for no other reason than so I can use them myself.

9

DETERMINING **LOCATIONS** AND USING **MAPS**

One of the chief benefits of building any mobile application is the ability to provide location-aware data to users. Android is no exception. Taking advantage of your user's location to help them make informed decisions should always be in the back of your mind. There is, however, a little to know about the basics of determining and using the device's location. I will show you a few tricks for speedy acquisition and then quickly show you how to display Android's built-in Google Maps view.

LOCATION BASICS

All location information on Android's systems is reached through Android's Location Manager class. There is, as you might have guessed, a permission requirement before you can access the user's location field.

MOTHER MAY I?

If you want to get the location of a user's device, you'll need to add the location permission to your manifest. Depending on the level of location data you want to acquire, you'll need to declare one of the following permissions:

```
<uses-permission
    android:name="android.permission.ACCESS_COARSE_LOCATION"/>
<uses-permission
    android:name="android.permission.ACCESS_FINE_LOCATION" />
```

The <uses-permission> tag should be declared inside the manifest but outside the <application> section.

BE CAREFUL WHAT YOU ASK FOR

Some users, bless their paranoid cotton socks, pay very close attention to the permissions you request in your manifest (each permission generates a warning when the app is purchased or downloaded from the Android Market). Several high-profile applications have been hit by negative reviews and user outrage for adding a location permission that didn't make sense. If you're going to use the location services on the device, make sure it's for the direct benefit of your users. Do otherwise, and your users *will* find out. Further, it's always a good idea to have a webpage that explains each permission you use. Those who care about it will find their way to it—and if they're informed, they will be less likely to complain.

FINDING A GOOD SUPPLIER

Your first step in using the location service, after you've added the permission of course, is finding a good supplier. Each device could have several different location services beyond the time- and power-consuming GPS system. Android allows you to specify criteria for the eventual provider you'll use. You do this by building a list of features you'd like and then asking Android for the one that best suits your needs. Here's a rather idealistic example I've put together using the getBestProvider method:

```
private String getBestProvider(LocationManager locationManager){
    Criteria criteria = new Criteria();
    criteria.setAccuracy(Criteria.ACCURACY_COARSE);
    criteria.setPowerRequirement(Criteria.POWER_LOW);
    criteria.setCostAllowed(false);
return locationManager.getBestProvider(criteria, true);
}
```

Before calling the getBestProvider method, you'll need to obtain a Location Manager object, which you can do with the following code:

```
locationManager = (LocationManager)getSystemService
    (Context.LOCATION_SERVICE);
```

Typically, I'll stash this pointer away somewhere so I never have to find it again.

GETTING THE GOODS

Once you've received the string ID for your ideal provider, you can register and start receiving location updates from the provider. Here's the code to register for updates:

```
locationManager.requestLocationUpdates(provider, 60000, 1000, this);
```

Calling this requestLocationUpdates method (which you'll need to define) will result in the onLocationChanged method being invoked every time the user's location is changed according to the criteria you set. Along with the provider string, you'll need to tell the system the minimum time between updates (in my case, 60 seconds—the documentation suggests not having it poll any faster than that), the minimum distance between intervals (in my case, 1000 meters), and the object that implements the LocationListener interface you want to receive callbacks. Here are the methods you're required to override:

```
public void onLocationChanged(final Location location) {}

@Override

public void onProviderDisabled(String provider) {}

@Override

public void onProviderEnabled(String provider) {}

@Override

public void onStatusChanged(String provider, int status,
→ Bundle extras) {}
```

The method I'm most interested in, in this case, is the onLocationChanged method. It will pass me that all-important location object. With that data, I can then call getLatitude and getLongitude. And with that, I know—with as much accuracy as possible—where in the world the device is.

Further, the LocationManager object contains an important static helper method called distanceBetween that will calculate the distance between geographic points. I point out this helper because I find myself using it all the time.

THE SNEAKY SHORTCUT

It can sometimes take many seconds for the location manager to spit out a user's location. There's a solution you can take advantage of to at least display an old value while the real location is being determined. You can, either before or after registering your listener, call getLastKnownLocation on your provider. This can provide some interesting results (especially if the device has spent a long time aloft in an airplane without an Internet connection), but it can often give the user something to look at or laugh at while you find their real location. You must, however, have defined the fine location permission to use this trick.

THAT'S IT!

As much as I would like to say that this is an incredibly complex operation, it's about as hard as tying your shoelaces. Given what you've been through up to this point, getting the location from the LocationManager should be a cakewalk. That said, I had my fair share of issues in writing the code for this chapter. If you are stumped, check the documentation and press on!

SHOW ME THE MAP!

FIGURE 9.1 Although strange, this is how your Android settings should look.

Determining your user's location is one thing, but actually putting those two indecipherable numbers (longitude and latitude) into context is where software gets a little more complex. Interestingly enough, the configuration needed to get a map onscreen is far more complex than the code to manipulate it. So, let's get started. If you want to follow along, go ahead and create a new Android project, and we'll start from there.

GETTING THE LIBRARY

The `MapActivity` and `MapView` are two classes available only in Google's API superset (APIs) of the Android SDK. In order to have access to them, you'll need to declare that your application uses the Google APIs library. You'll need to download this super-library (the same way you got the Ice Cream Sandwich and Gingerbread SDKs back in Chapter 1). **Figure 9.1** shows what the settings screen for your project should look like if you've got it dialed in correctly.

Once you've set up your SDK values correctly, there are a few things in the manifest I need to talk with you about.

ADDING TO THE MANIFEST

There are two critical things that, through the manifest, you need to tell the system. The first is that your application uses the Google Maps library. The second is that you need permission to access the Internet. While you will not have to call anything directly to get online, the map view will. Here's what the tail end of your manifest should look like with these two additions:

```
<manifest> <!--Rest of the manifest omiited here for brevity.-->
    <application>
        <activity>
        </activity>
    <uses-library android:name="com.google.android.maps" />
    </application>
    <uses-permission android:name="android.permission.INTERNET"/>
</manifest>
```

Again, you're telling Android that

■ You'll be referencing the Google Maps libraries.

■ You need permission to access the Internet.

Now, with that out of the way, it's time to switch your boring Activity to a bigger, sexier MapActivity class.

CREATING THE MAPACTIVITY

Switching your default activity to a map activity requires you to add the appropriate Java include path and a required method. When you're finished, it will look something like this:

```
public class MapsExampleProjectActivity extends MapActivity {
    @Override
    public void onCreate(Bundle savedInstanceState) {
        super.onCreate(savedInstanceState);
        setContentView(R.layout.main);
    }
    @Override
    protected boolean isRouteDisplayed() {
        return false;
    }
}
```

Now that you have your Activity class switched over to the MapActivity class, you can add a MapView to your main.xml layout file.

CREATING A MAPVIEW

This is the view into which Android will draw its map tiles. It behaves exactly like any other view, with one notable exception: You need an API key to access Google Maps.

PLACING THE MAPVIEW

Here's what my simple main.xml file looks like right now:

```
<?xml version="1.0" encoding="utf-8"?>

<LinearLayout xmlns:android="http://schemas.android.com/
→  apk/res/android"

    android:layout_width="fill_parent"

    android:layout_height="fill_parent"

    android:orientation="vertical" >

    <com.google.android.maps.MapView

        android:id="@+id/map_view"

        android:clickable="true"

        android:layout_width="fill_parent"

        android:layout_height="fill_parent"

        android:apiKey="your API key goes in this field"

/>

</LinearLayout>
```

As you can see, I've placed my map view as the only one onscreen. You can actually place it anywhere you want, just as you would position any other view. Further, it doesn't require, as the ListActivity does, a special reserved Android ID. Let me show you where to get the value that you'll place in the apiKey field.

SIGNING UP FOR A MAP KEY

Getting a map key is pretty easy. Head over to http://code.google.com/android/maps-api-signup.html and run the command they suggest:

```
keytool -list -keystore ~/.android/debug.keystore
```

From the sign-up page, you must agree to their terms (which you should probably read first), enter the output from your keytool command, and get your API key. Toss that string into the apiKey section (the highlighted line in the main.xml code) of the MapView, and you're good to go. Remember, the map key is bound to whatever key you signed your .apk with (in this case, the debugging one). When you sign your .apk for release, you'll need to remember to generate a new key for it.

TIP: If the keytool asks for a password, the default is "android."

RUN, BABY, RUN

You've configured everything, dotted all your i's, and crossed all your t's. It's time to take this map view out for a spin. When it comes time to move and render the map, you'll be primarily interfacing with the MapControl, which you'll actually retrieve from the map view itself. The simple work for my example is all done in my sample code's onCreate method:

```java
MapView mv;

MapController controller;

@Override
    public void onCreate(Bundle savedInstanceState) {
        super.onCreate(savedInstanceState);
        setContentView(R.layout.main);
        mv = (MapView)findViewById(R.id.map_view);
        controller = mv.getController();
        GeoPoint point = new GeoPoint((int)(40.734641 * 1e6),
          (int)(-73.996181 * 1e6));
        controller.animateTo(point);
        controller.setZoom(12);
    }
```

FIGURE 9.2 New York City. The biggest small town you'll ever know.

In this code, I'm doing a few important things:

1. Retrieving the `MapView` from my layout with the inimitable `findViewById` method.

2. Obtaining and manipulating the `MapController`.

3. Creating a new `GeoPoint` on which to center the map view.

The location listed in the example happens to be New York City (where I'm currently writing this book), and I've set the zoom level high enough that you can almost see my house—all right, maybe not! **Figure 9.2** shows what all your hard work thus far has yielded.

GeoPoints

Google, in its not-so-infinite wisdom, decided that GeoPoints for the map view should not accept latitude and longitude values in degrees like every other API in the SDK. Instead, they take them in 1e6 values. This means, simply, that you must multiply any latitude or longitude value you wish to reference in the map view by 1e6 before handing off. Interesting map errors will result if you forget this step.

WRAPPING **UP**

In this chapter, I showed you the very basics for finding a device's location and displaying a map onscreen. If you're looking to go further into this topic, you should explore map overlays through the OverlayItem class. Overlays let you point out specific locations (addresses, businesses, or cat pictures) to your users.

As always, be very careful what kind of location services you use, especially while the user is not in your application. Nothing will drain a user's battery faster—and make them angrier—than heavy locational lookups in the background. If you're planning a very location-heavy application, be sure to do LOTS of battery-draw testing before you release it. Your users and your application's ratings will be much happier for it.

FRAGMENTS

Fragments, conceptually, are like activities with a slightly more complex lifecycle. They can be given a screen to themselves if there isn't much room, or they can be placed with many other fragments on a larger tablet screen. An activity can contain any number of fragments. In this way, the Android SDK allows you to expand and collapse the views in your application to take advantage of more and less screen space. There is one thing that the activity can do that the fragment cannot—namely, the activity can register for intents in the manifest; fragments rely on their host activity to pass on launch information. Further, it's important to implement fragments such that they are totally unaware of what other fragments are visible. This becomes important, because you'll want to change that configuration depending on how much space you have.

If you're planning on coding along with me in this chapter, make sure you have a project that is set to version 3.0 or higher of the Android SDK (API Level 11 or greater).

THE LIFECYCLE OF THE FRAGMENT

Fragments have fairly complex lifecycles. There are many methods to explore, but onCreateView must be implemented for the fragment to appear onscreen. onCreate View is your fragment's one chance to create a view to display onscreen. If you fail to return a view to the system, your application will crash and burn.

Here is the startup lifecycle; the methods are listed in the order the system will call them:

- onAttach. This is called when your fragment is attaching to an activity.

- onCreate. This is called when the fragment is being initialized. This is a great place to initialize any variables you'll need later.

- onCreateView. This is your opportunity to create and return the fragment's root view. This is the first method that will be called if your fragment is returning to the screen after having been previously paused.

- onStart. Similar to the same call on the activity, this is called when the fragment is about to be placed onscreen.

- onResume. This is called when the fragment is back onscreen.

At this point, your fragment is frolicking on the screen, receiving touch and key events, or just hanging around and looking great. If the user leaves the screen or switches to a view that no longer includes the fragment, the following shutdown lifecycle will take place:

- onPause. This is called if the fragment is removed from the screen or the user presses the home button. This is the only part of the shutdown lifecycle you're guaranteed to get (it would be the only method you get in the rare situation that your application is put in the background and then your process is killed due to resource constraints). onPause is the best time for you to save any data or state information that you want the user to be able to see when the fragment is resumed later.

- onStop. Similar to the activity's version of this method, onStop is called when your fragment has left the screen. It tends to be called in conjunction with the activity's onStop method.

- onDestroyView. This is your last chance to pull data out of the views before they go away.

- onDestroy. This is called when the fragment is being removed from the screen and will not return. This is the time to make sure all your threads are stopped, loaders are canceled, and any broadcast receivers are unregistered.

- onDetach. Called as the fragment loses its association with an activity, onDetach is the last of your methods the system will call before the fragment heads to the great garbage collector in the sky.

CREATING A FRAGMENT

To create a fragment, you'll need to make a Java class that extends the Fragment class. An incredibly simple implementation would look something like this:

```java
public class ContentFragment extends Fragment{
    @Override
    public View onCreateView(LayoutInflater inflater,
        ViewGroup container, Bundle savedInstanceState) {
        View v = inflater.inflate(R.layout.content_layout, null);
    }
}
```

Fragments, of course, need their own layouts to show anything onscreen. This ContentFragment class will just show a simple text view. Here is the content_layout.xml file whose contents will be drawn as the fragment itself:

```xml
<?xml version="1.0" encoding="utf-8"?>
<LinearLayout xmlns:android="http://schemas.android.com/
    apk/res/android"
    android:layout_width="match_parent"
    android:layout_height="match_parent"
    android:orientation="vertical" >
    <TextView
        android:layout_width="match_parent"
        android:layout_height="match_parent"
        android:id="@+id/content_text_view"
        />
</LinearLayout>
```

With the XML layout file and the new ContentFragment class, you'll have a very basic but functional fragment for displaying text on the screen. Later methods can call the fragment's getView method and findViewById on that view to get and modify the required child views. Here's what a method to change the contents of the text view might look like:

```
private void setContentText(String text){
    TextView tv =
(TextView)getView().findViewById(R.id.content_text_view);
    tv.setText(text);
}
```

Keep in mind, however, that the getView method works only after you've returned from onCreateView. While you now have a fully functioning fragment, you still need to make it appear onscreen.

SHOWING A FRAGMENT

There are two main ways one can make fragments appear onscreen.

USING XML
You can declare a fragment in an XML layout to make the fragment appear onscreen, like so:

```
File: res/layout/content_activity_layout.xml

<?xml version="1.0" encoding="utf-8"?>

<LinearLayout xmlns:android="http://schemas.android.com/
    apk/res/android"
    android:layout_width="fill_parent"
    android:layout_height="fill_parent"
    android:orientation="vertical" >
    <fragment android:name="com.haseman.fragments.ContentFragment"
        android:layout_width="match_parent"
```

```
        android:layout_height="match_parent"
        android:id="@+id/list_fragment"/>
</LinearLayout>
```

This layout can then be set as the content view for a FragmentActivity, like so:

```
public class ContentViewingActivity extends FragmentActivity{
    public void onCreate(Bundle data){
        super.onCreate(data);
        setContentView(R.layout.content_activity_layout);
    }
}
```

Figure 10.1 shows the results of using XML to make the fragment appear onscreen.

THE FragmentActivity CLASS

The FragmentActivty is a special class you'll need to use only if you want to work with fragments on versions of Android earlier than 3.0. For Honeycomb and Ice Cream Sandwich, a simple activity contains all the pieces you need to interact with fragments. You can find the FragmentActivity class in the Android compatibility library.

FIGURE 10.1 A fragment with a single text view.

Fragments, when set up this way, can be placed onscreen the same way as views. Here's an XML layout to show a list view with the text view next to it:

```xml
<?xml version="1.0" encoding="utf-8"?>
<LinearLayout xmlns:android="http://schemas.android.com/
→  apk/res/android"
    android:layout_width="fill_parent"
    android:layout_height="fill_parent"
    android:orientation="horizontal" >
    <fragment android:name="com.haseman.fragments.DemoListFragment"
        android:layout_width="0dp"
        android:layout_height="match_parent"
        android:id="@+id/list_fragment"
        android:layout_weight=".33"/>
    <fragment android:name="com.haseman.fragments.ContentFragment"
        android:layout_width="0dp"
        android:layout_height="match_parent"
        android:id="@+id/content_fragment"
        android:layout_weight=".66"/>
</LinearLayout>
```

I've used a linear layout and some weighting in the fragments to give the Demo ListFragment the left one-third of the screen and the ContentFragment the right two-thirds. (If you're wondering about DemoListFragment, you can find it in the sample code for this chapter.)

Figure 10.2 shows what it looks like on a tablet.

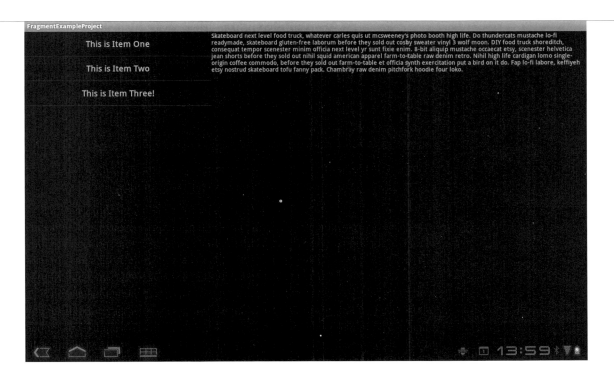

FragmentExampleProject

This is Item One

This is Item Two

This is Item Three!

Skateboard next level food truck, whatever carles quis ut mcsweeney's photo booth high life. Do thundercats mustache lo-fi readymade, skateboard gluten-free laborum before they sold out cosby sweater vinyl 3 wolf moon. DIY food truck shoreditch, consequat tempor scenester minim officia next level yr sunt fixie enim. 8-bit aliquip mustache occaecat etsy, scenester helvetica jean shorts before they sold out nihil squid american apparel farm-to-table raw denim retro. Nihil high life cardigan lomo single-origin coffee commodo, before they sold out farm-to-table et officia synth exercitation put a bird on it do. Fap lo-fi labore, keffiyeh etsy nostrud skateboard tofu fanny pack. Chambray raw denim pitchfork hoodie four loko.

13:59

FIGURE 10.2 Two fragments on one screen.

USING THE FRAGMENT MANAGER

Although being able to lay out fragments in the XML files is great, you'll want to be able to interact with the fragments on your screen at runtime as well. For this, you'll use the FragmentManager, which is Android's tool to manipulate fragments.

Getting a fragment manager on Honeycomb and later requires you to call get FragmentManager. Getting a fragment manager for earlier devices requires you to call getSupportFragmentManager from a FragmentActivity.

You can add fragments to the screen programmatically with the following code:

```
FragmentManager manager = getSupportFragmentManager();

FragmentTransaction ft = manager.beginTransaction();

ft.add(containerViewId, new DemoListFragment());

ft.commit();
```

The variable `containerViewId` should refer to an existing `ViewGroup` in your activity's layout where the new fragment should be placed. You can also, at a later time, replace one fragment with another by calling `replace(containerViewId, newFragment);`, where `containerViewId` specifies the view container that currently holds the fragment you'd like to replace. You can replace only fragments that were previously added using a `FragmentManager` transaction; fragments declared statically in XML layouts cannot be replaced.

By using either XML or the fragment manager to set up and modify views, you should have no trouble building complex, scalable, and beautiful applications that render well on both handsets and tablets.

Remember that all fragments should work independently of their siblings (much in the same way that activities should stay independent), even if they might share the same screen.

Given the power of Android's layout folders (which we covered at length in Chapters 3 and 7), you should see the possibilities in building one layout for tablets (which could have several fragments on it) and building another for small-screened phones (which would have only one visible fragment at a time).

If you're looking for a simple example, I highly recommend you take a look at the project in the sample code for this chapter.

PROVIDING BACKWARD COMPATIBILITY

Android has, thankfully, bundled fragments into their compatibility library. This means you can work with fragments even if you're planning on supporting pre-3.0 devices. I highly recommend that you use it whenever you can. Installing it is as simple as clicking the menu item shown in **Figure 10.3**.

Take note, however, that building your project against a 3.0 or higher version and still using the compatibility libraries at the same time can get a little complicated. If you're doing this, make sure all your imports come from the support library like this:

```
import android.support.v4.app.Fragment;
```

instead of like this:

```
import android.app.Fragment;
```

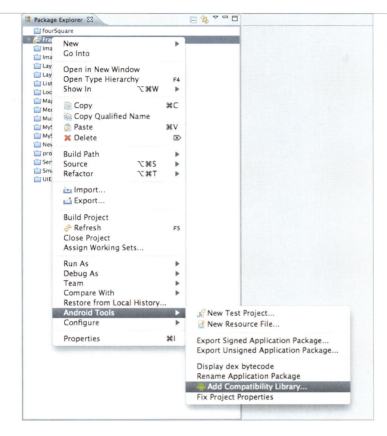

FIGURE 10.3 Installing the compatibility library.

Using the support library will ensure that your application will run correctly on newer and older systems alike.

Further, if you're planning on using the compatibility library and fragments, remember that you'll need to use a FragmentActivity instead of a regular Activity.

With the compatibility support and the dynamic nature of fragments, it becomes quite possible to create an application with a great interaction model that works well on both phones and tablets. I don't have time to spell it all out here, but there is sample code for achieving this in the companion source code for this chapter. Remember what you've read here, and take a look through it.

THE **ACTION** BAR

FIGURE 10.4 A basic action bar.

With the transition from Android 2.3 to 3.0, Google has eliminated both the search button and the menu key. From personal experience, I can tell you that many new users never find functionality that is placed in the options menu. Its removal from the system is, indeed, a very good thing.

Google, bless their expensive cotton socks, has moved the icons that used to reside in the options menu to the action bar. Further, you can specify a search view in the action bar (to replace the search button). This takes up more screen space, but on a tablet (and on later phones), there is more than enough space to go around.

The action bar now represents the primary way your users will navigate through your Honeycomb or Ice Cream Sandwich application. Sadly, this new tool is available only through versions 3.0 (target 11) or later. It would require a fair amount of typing, but it's very possible to emulate the action bar on earlier systems by using a simple linear layout and a few image views. You are, however, on your own to implement it. There is no support for the action bar in the compatibility library.

SHOWING THE ACTION BAR

Since the action bar is supported only in SDK versions 3.0 and later, your manifest will have to explicitly declare that it supports target 11 or greater.

```
<uses-sdk android:minSdkVersion="7"
    android:targetSdkVersion="11"
    />
```

At this point, when your project is built and run on any Honeycomb and later system, you should see a basic version of the action bar containing your application's icon and the default title of the activity (**Figure 10.4**).

ADDING ELEMENTS TO THE ACTION BAR

In addition to allowing you to set your own title with a call to `setTitle`, the action bar can handle three different types of objects:

- Icons. Both in a drop-down menu on the right-hand side and as actionable items in the bar itself.

- Tabs. Buttons along the top, built to manipulate fragments on the screen.

- Action views. Search boxes and drop-down lists (for things like sort orders, account selection, or death-ray intensities).

Further, Android will always make your application icon (farthest to the left) clickable. It is expected that tapping this icon will, by default, return the user to your application's home screen (whatever this means to your application's behavior). You can also visually indicate that the home icon will go one level back in the activity stack by calling `setDisplayHomeAsUpEnabled(true)`.

The way you make changes to what's in the action bar is very similar to how you used to interact with the options menu. This is not by accident. Because the action bar is supposed to replace the options menu, you call methods and configure files similarly to how you used to deal with the menu. This also makes it easy to gracefully degrade service to phones on older versions of the Android SDK.

ADDING AN ICON

Icons are most easily placed in the action bar by extending `onCreateOptionsMenu` and adding the menu icons you'd like. I've added a delete icon to the action bar with the following code:

```
@Override
public boolean onCreateOptionsMenu(Menu menu){
    MenuItem item = menu.add("delete");
    item.setIcon(android.R.drawable.ic_delete);
    if(Build.VERSION.SDK_INT >= 11){
        item.setShowAsAction(MenuItem.SHOW_AS_ACTION_IF_ROOM);
    }
    return true;
}
```

FIGURE 10.5 Adding an
action icon.

FIGURE 10.6 A non-action icon.

If the Android SDK is greater than 3.0, the system will call this method when the activity is starting (so it can build the action bar). You'll notice that I'm calling setShowAsAction only if we're running on Honeycomb or later. **Figure 10.5** shows what the action bar looks like on a handset running Ice Cream Sandwich.

If you omit the call to setShowAsAction on a Honeycomb tablet, you'll see an options menu icon that contains the menu item on the right side. On Ice Cream Sandwich, it will move the menu item to a more traditional contextual menu. **Figure 10.6** shows what it looks like on a tablet after I've clicked it.

REACTING TO ICON CLICKS

When the user clicks one of your action bar icons, Android will call your implementation of the onOptionsItemSelected method. Here's my very simple example method:

```
public boolean onOptionsItemSelected(MenuItem item){
    int id = item.getItemId();
    if(id == android.R.id.home){
        //The user clicked the left-hand app icon.
    //As this is the home screen, ignore it.
        return true;
    }
    else{
        //Perform the delete action here
        return true;
    }
}
```

With that, you should have the basics of creating both options menu and action bar icons. Alternatively, you can declare your icons as XML files and inflate them using the MenuInflater. Check the documentation (http://developer.android.com/guide/topics/ui/menus.html) for a complete rundown on how to use XML files in /res/menu to streamline the process.

FIGURE 10.7 A tab bar in Google Calendar.

ADDING A TAB

Placing a tab in the action bar is a totally different process. You'll use the ActionBar class itself to add them. Further, you'll need to implement an ActionBar.Tab Listener (it tells the system, through a series of overridden methods, what to do when the tab is tapped by the user).

Once you've implemented your listener, you should then add the following code to your activity's onCreate method:

```
ActionBar bar = getActionBar();

bar.setNavigationMode(ActionBar.NAVIGATION_MODE_TABS);

ActionBar.Tab tab1 = bar.newTab();

tab1.setText("Tab Text");

tab1.setTabListener(new ExampleTabListener());

bar.addTab(tab1);
```

For each tab you'd like to add, you must go through the process of requesting a new tab from the action bar, setting the listener, and then adding it to the action bar. **Figure 10.7** shows a great-looking example of a tab bar in the Google Calendar application.

Each tab will trigger different events on the fragments within an activity. For the Google Calendar application, it will hide and show the various ways in which the user could view their calendar.

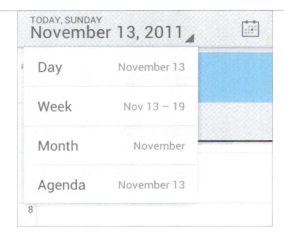

FIGURE 10.8 A drop-down list action view.

USING ACTION VIEWS

Action views (like search and menu drop-downs) are somewhat complex and thus are impossible to go into in great detail here. You can use them to add search fields (as there is no longer a hard search button in Honeycomb and beyond) as well as drop-down menus. **Figure 10.8** shows the same calendar picker implemented as a drop-down menu on a phone running Ice Cream Sandwich.

For more information on how to make drop-down lists, search fields, and even your own custom views, check the `ActionBar` documentation at http://developer .android.com/guide/topics/ui/actionbar.html.

WRAPPING UP

As you can see, Google has been very busy building new user interface paradigms for tablets in Honeycomb. Once they settled on how to make the tablets work, they added those new UI methods to the telephone world with Ice Cream Sandwich.

Using the action bar, Google was able to do away with two hard menu buttons (options menu and search), while keeping those concepts active in the user experience. The options menu button was replaced by icons added to the action bar, and the search button was replaced by the ability to add custom action views to that very same bar.

With fragments, Google has enabled us to place more or less on the screen as the available real estate shifts between devices. Through fragments, we are no longer limited to having one *thing* on the screen at any given time. However, if we need to handle smaller screens, fragments make it easy to shift back into the one-thing-per-screen layout.

Fragments and the action bar are very new concepts, and it's clear that Android developers are still trying to figure out how best to use them. Please, help us to push the mobile user experience forward by implementing your own killer user interfaces using these new toys Google has given us.

11

PUBLISHING YOUR APPLICATION

For the most part, the Android Market is one of the easiest-to-use application stores I've ever encountered. But although you can update an application almost instantly without any of the hassles of other app stores, there are still a few things you should be aware of before you publish. We'll cover packaging, versioning, and creating a release build.

PACKAGING AND VERSIONING

There are a few key points in your manifest that you need to pay attention to before you consider producing a release build to go to market. You'll need to make sure your application isn't debuggable (not so much an issue with newer versions of the Android client). You'll also want to make sure your package name is unique and consistent in each subsequent version. Last, there are two fields to pay attention to when upgrading an existing application. Let's take a closer look at all three.

PREVENTING DEBUGGING

Shipping your application out the door with debugging enabled will allow anyone with a micro USB cable to step through lines of code in your app, look at the contents of variables, and do other things that no security-aware engineer would like to have happen. The debugging flag is turned off by default, but if you've turned it on, it will appear in the application portion of the manifest:

```
<application
    android:icon="@drawable/ic_launcher"
    android:label="@string/app_name"
    android:debuggable="true">
```

When the application ships, make sure that you either remove the line entirely or set the following:

```
android:debuggable="false"
```

NAMING THE PACKAGE

The package you declare in your manifest can, for the most part, contain almost any string you fancy. I've highlighted one from a previous example here:

```
<?xml version="1.0" encoding="utf-8"?>
<manifest xmlns:android="http://schemas.android.com/apk/res/android"
    package="com.haseman.layouts"
    android:versionCode="1"
    android:versionName="1.0">
```

Although I named this package to correspond to my layouts example, you could just as easily declare a package like

```
package="com.sparkle.pants.fairy.dust.unicorn"
```

I wouldn't recommend using the unicorn example (it's somewhat outrageous), but the fact remains that you can. However, the package name you choose must be different from all other existing packages in the entire Android Market. Be sure it's unique and that it's something you can live with for as long as you upgrade the application. When you upgrade your app, it absolutely must have the same package name as the build that came before it. Typically, the naming convention goes something like `com.company_name.product_name`. But again, the package name for your application is entirely up to you.

VERSIONING

There are two values to pay attention to when updating an existing application. First, you should (but are not required to) increase the value inside the `versionName` field of the manifest declaration. Standard rules for the version number apply: Major releases get a new primary number (1.0 to 2.0), while small patches should get a secondary bump (1.0 to 1.1). The version name is what shows to the user in the Android Market and in your application's details screen. The version name is "1.0" in the previous example's manifest file.

The field you *must* pay careful attention to is `versionCode`. This is the value that must change every time you do an update for the Android Market. Sending an update to the Android Market will be rejected unless you change the `versionCode`. Typically, Android developers will make the version code by taking the periods out of the version name and padding each portion of the name to create a two-digit number for each section. The number must be unique, but it does not necessarily have to be sequential. So version 1.0.1 would become 010001, and 2.3.12 would become 020312. This is a pretty basic way to make sure your version names stay tied to the version code without much complexity. It's a good idea to make this number constantly grow even though, according to the documentation, it isn't technically required to. However, adopting a convention of incrementing the numbers ensures it will be unique.

SETTING A MINIMUM SDK VALUE

The Android Market requires that you specify a minimum SDK value for your application. You can do this in the manifest by including the uses-sdk field, like so:

```
<?xml version="1.0" encoding="utf-8"?>
<manifest xmlns:android="http://schemas.android.com/apk/res/android"
    package="com.haseman.location"
    android:versionCode="1"
    android:versionName="1.0">
    <uses-sdk android:minSdkVersion="7"/>
    <!-- The rest of your application goes here-->
</manifest>
```

The number in minSdkVersion corresponds to the integer value for the SDK. In this case, by declaring version 7, I'm not allowing phones earlier than the Android 2.1 update 1 (which is SDK version 7) to install my application. Be sure to test your application on the versions you support, even if you just test it briefly with an emulator.

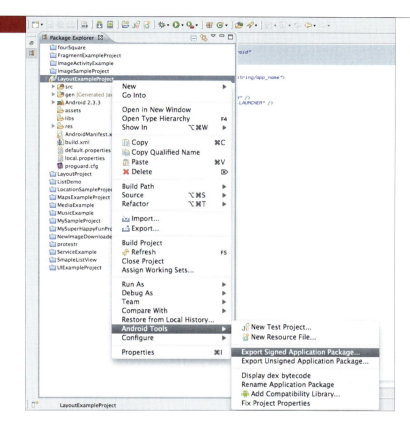

FIGURE 11.1 Exporting a release build.

So your version number is sorted, your code is tested, and all your resources are in place—it's time to make a release build before submitting.

There are two ways you can go about producing your final APK: through Apache's ant (which will build your application from the command line in conjunction with the build.xml file) or through Eclipse's Android tools. If you're comfortable with the command line, I'm going to assume you can create a release build on your own. In this chapter, I'll focus on creating your release build through Eclipse.

EXPORTING A SIGNED BUILD

The Eclipse tools make it very easy to produce an effective release build. Simply right-click your project in the Package Explorer, and choose Android Tools > Export Signed Application Package (**Figure 11.1**).

You'll be asked if you want to use an existing keystore file or create a new one. Because this is your first time releasing your product, you'll need to create a new one. Enter a location for the file, or click the Browse button to find one. Enter a password, and re-enter it to confirm that it is correctly typed (**Figure 11.2**). The *keystore* is a file that can contain any number of keys. For your purposes, you'll only really need one key. All your applications can be signed with the same one, or you can use different keys—it's up to you (but I recommend using only one, because it's less to keep track of).

BACKING UP YOUR KEYSTORE FILE

I'll say it again: **Back up your keystore file**. If I could invent a way to make an HTML `<blink>` tag in a printed book, I would do it here. The Android Market will not let you upgrade an application if you haven't signed it with the same key. If you lose the keystore file you've just created, you'll never be able to upgrade your application. Burn it to a disk, and store the disk somewhere other than your house. Save it in the cloud (Amazon S3, Dropbox, your mother's house) in as many safe places as you can.

Once you've created your keystore, Eclipse will ask you to create a key. You aren't required to fill in all the lower fields. If you do, however, you should probably take it a little more seriously than I did in **Figure 11.3**.

FIGURE 11.2 Creating a keystore file.

FIGURE 11.3 Creating a key.

You'll be creating a key (to place in your new keystore file) that requires an alias and its own password.

Be sure that you make the number you use for the Validity field large enough to be valid for a very, very long time. You never know, Android could still be around one thousand years from now. It pays to be prepared. Last, you'll need to fill out at least one of the several remaining fields, but I recommend you fill in as many as apply.

Click Next to create your key. You'll just need to tell Eclipse where to put your APK, and you're finished!

REMEMBER TO ZIPALIGN

For you command-line users, one thing that Eclipse is doing for its users is a tool called Zipalign (found in the `tools/` folder of the SDK). Zipalign decreases your application's load times. If you're using the Eclipse tools, it's already happening for you automatically. If you aren't using Eclipse, make sure you take this step on the command line after you've signed the build. It's speed for free, so make sure you take advantage of it.

SUBMITTING YOUR BUILD

At this point, it's time to sign up for a developer account and submit your build. Android's application submission page is fairly self-explanatory, but I should point out that it's important to provide the Market with as many screenshots, videos, and graphical assets as you have time to generate. Making the decision to purchase an application can, if you can believe it, be a difficult one. Users need to be able to trust that your application actually works as advertised, so giving them a sneak peek is essential.

WATCH YOUR CRASH REPORTS AND FIX THEM

The marketplace provides a very helpful capability: Users, when they experience a crash, have the option of reporting that crash to you. Take advantage of it as much as possible. Get in touch with users, and fix absolutely everything you can. When you get stuck, go online and use every resource available (your favorite search engine, Google Groups, or Stack Overflow, to name a few). If you're seeing a crash you don't understand, chances are high that other developers have battled the same thing; we're a very helpful bunch.

UPDATE FREQUENTLY

Your application, after you submit it, will show up in the Market within hours. This allows you to frequently update in order to add small features, fix bugs, and make small tweaks. No other platform allows you this kind of speed from submission to availability. Use it. You'll be amazed by how grateful your users will be if you respond to their problems quickly.

WRAPPING **UP**

In parting, I want to give you one more piece of advice: Make a meaningful contribution to the Android landscape. While you'll undoubtedly have questions that this book cannot answer, you now have the vocabulary and knowledge that will allow you to find answers. This means you have no excuse but to make something amazing. Please—the Android Market is, for lack of a better phrase, full of crap. The world doesn't need another flatulence app; we need things that make data more accessible, meaningful, fun, useful, and interesting. Do not build apps, build applications.

Good luck, and happy hacking.

INDEX

onDestroyView method, 223
onDetach method, 223
onPause method, 223
onResume method, 222
onStart method, 222
onStop method, 223
placing onscreen, 228–230
showing, 225–230
text view, 225, 227

G

GeoPoints, using with maps, 219
getApplication method, 50
Google Maps library, 214, 216
gray background, adding to RelativeLayout, 95–96

H

hierarchy viewer, locating, xv
Honeycomb
    action bar, 232
    action views, 236
    FragmentActivity class, 226
    FragmentManager, 229
    Navigation, 232
    SetShowAsAction, 234

I

Ice Cream Sandwich
    action bar, 232
    FragmentActivity class, 226
    Navigation, 232
icon clicks, reacting to, 234–235
icons, adding to action bar, 233–234
image fetcher
    handleIntent method, 116–117
    implementing, 116–117
image uploading, automatic, 150–151
ImageIntentService, 114
imageReceiver class, 119–120

images
    cache folder, 115
    downloading and displaying, 100–101
    external storage, 115
    fetching, 114–120
    listener for result broadcast, 118–119
    notifyFinished method, 118
    rendering download, 118–120
<include> tag, using for small changes, 172–176
installing
    Android SDK for Linux users, 6
    Android SDK for Mac users, 5–6
    Android SDK for Windows users, 6
    Eclipse IDE, 5
Intent class manifest registration, 37–38
intent filters, registering for, 40
intent-based communication, 150–159
    auto image uploading, 150–151
    declaring services, 151
    getting services, 151
    going to foreground, 155–157
    observing content changes, 158–159
    spinning up services, 154–155
    starting services, 152–154
intents. See also activities
    adding, 38–40
    BroadcastReceiver, 41–43
    creating, 29–30
    features of, 37
    getting for activities, 31
    listening for, 41–45
    listening for information, 43
    moving data, 45–47
    receivers, 41–43
    receiving, 37
    registering receivers, 42–43
    retrieving and using strings, 46–47
    reviewing, 47
    self-contained BroadcastReceivers, 44
    stopping listening, 43
    toasts, 42

R.javafile
  code, 72
  creation of, 71

S

saving files to SD cards, 116
screen layout, creating for activities, 27–29
screen sizes, handling, 75, 89
screens, defining in layout-land folder, 177–178
SD card, saving files to, 116
SDK (software development kit)
  downloading, xiv, 4
  installing for Linux users, 6
  installing for Mac users, 5–6
  installing for Windows users, 6
SDK methods, accessing with reflection, 183–184
SDK value, setting, 242
SDK version number
  declaring support for, 181
  finding, 184
Service class
  described, 148
  onBind method, 151
ServiceExampleActivity, 152–153
services. *See also* communication
  binding and communicating with, 164–165
  bringing into foreground, 155
  colon (:) in process, 161
  ContentObserver, 158
  Context.stopService, 149
  creating, 161–162
  creating notifications, 155–156
  cursor for ContentProvider, 159
  declaring, 113–114, 151
  getting, 151
  ImageIntentService, 114
  IMusicService.Stub class, 164
  keeping running, 149
  lifecycle, 148
  main thread, 149
  Notification object, 156

notification pull-down, 157
  onBind method, 148
  onClickListener, 164
  onCreate method, 148
  onDestroy method, 149
  onStartCommand method, 148
  setForegroundState method, 155–156
  shutting down, 149
  as singletons, 148
  Start and Stop buttons, 152
  startForeground method, 149
  starting, 152–154
  stopSelf method, 149
setContentView method, 28, 33, 55
setForegroundState method
  music playback, 203
  using, 155–156
SharedPreferences, apply method, 182
signed build
  exporting, 243–244
  keystore file, 244
sound effects, playing, 196–197
Start and Stop buttons, adding to services, 152
StrictMode.enableDefaults, 120

T

tabs, adding to action bars, 235
text view
  customizing, 65–66
  grabbing instance of, 59–60
TextView class, 142–143
TextView ID, creating for activities, 27
thread violations, spotting, 120. *See also* main thread
Toast API, 42
troubleshooting emulator, 18–19
Twitter data, creating for list views, 136–138
Twitter feed
  displaying, 143
  downloading, 143
  parsing, 143
TwitterAsyncTask, 136–138